AA POCKET GUIDE

CALIFORNIA

**Written by Carole Chester
Peace and Quiet section
by Paul Sterry**

© The Automobile Association
1995
First published 1990 as *Essential
California*
Revised second edition 1992
Revised third edition 1995
Reprinted March 1997
Reprinted as *Pocket Guide
California* 1999
Reprinted 2000

Maps © The Automobile
Association 1995, 2000

Published by AA Publishing, a
trading name of Automobile
Association Developments
Limited, whose registered office is
Norfolk House, Priestley Road,
Basingstoke, Hampshire
RG24 9NY.
Registered number 1878835.

Distributed in the United Kingdom
by AA Publishing, Norfolk House,
Priestley Road, Basingstoke,
Hampshire RG24 9NY.

A CIP catalogue record for this
book is available from the British
Library.

ISBN 0 7495 2113 9

Colour separation: L C Repro Ltd,
Aldermaston.

Printed by: Printer Trento srl, Italy

Front cover picture: *Golden Gate
Bridge* (AA Photo Library –
K Paterson)

Contents

This book employs a simple
rating system to help choose
which places to visit:

✓	'top ten'

♦♦♦ do not miss
♦♦   see if you can
♦   worth seeing if you
     have time

Inyo National Forest. Millions of acres of breathtaking Californian wilderness are protected in National Parks or Forests

INTRODUCTION

There is something about California that sparks the imagination! You can't help but associate it with sunny colours and attitudes, golden bodies and a laid-back style of life. We eat the fruit from California – Christmas dates and out-of-season strawberries – and we drink the wine – the chardonnays and cabernets. We watch the films made in California – the old ones when Hollywood was in its heyday, and the new ones, perhaps from Universal Studios Hollywood. We even find California's flashy fancies and fashions lovable; it's the ideal setting for Disneyland! Here Out West, where the lure of gold brought the original settlers, they do things a little differently. Here Out West, movie stars have become mayors – one was even an American president. Today's local crazes are tomorrow's world-wide. Fads – from the 1960s penchant for psychedelia to the health-conscious 1990s no-smoking regulations – are taken seriously. But Californians are always fun to be with.

Whatever you want to find, you *will* find in this narrow state locked between mountains and sea. You will find slick, sophisticated cities like Los Angeles and San Francisco, full of round-the-clock action, yet out along the highways you'll also find smalltown camaraderie and hospitality. You can discover that life blooms in the desert where communities and mega resorts have mushroomed around the green oasis of Palm Springs. You can linger in the vine-clad valleys of the Napa and Russian Rivers, and ride or climb up the Sierra Mountains. California's Great Outdoors is tempting. In addition to its celebrated beaches, the state boasts national forests and parks of outstanding beauty, well equipped for tourists. And the sporty won't have to travel far to find a tennis-court or golf course, hot-air ballooning or good boating waters. Yet this region is not lacking in history – long before the wagon trains rolled, the Spanish had built a chain of Missions between San Diego and Sonoma, many still in existence today. San Diego itself, the birthplace of California, was discovered in the 16th century.

History – and tomorrowland – in one. The state's first capital, for example, San José, today boasts a population of over half a million and, with surrounding Santa Clara Valley, is a world leader in the microchip industry. There is such a concentration of electronic technology firms that the area has been dubbed 'Silicon Valley'. Tomorrowland was also dreamed up by Walt Disney, who

The other California – the hi-tech world of Silicon Valley, around the former state capital of San José

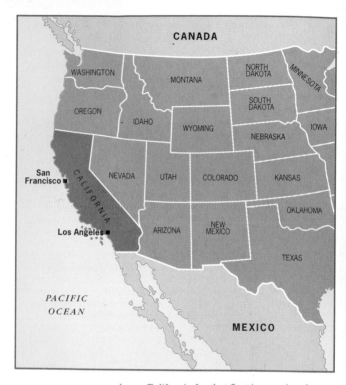

chose California for that first innovative theme park. What other country (or state for that matter) hasn't tried to copy the Disney technique, project the Disney magic – without the Disney team, without its success.
Claims to fame are multifold but true for the Golden State – the United States' second highest mountain (Whitney) and lowest, hottest point (Death Valley), and the world's tallest and largest trees (the redwoods and sequoias). It has some of America's longest ski runs and some of the largest man-made lakes; it has some of the country's finest and longest-established hotels and restaurants; it has been home to some of the United States' wealthiest citizens and best-known personalities. How can you afford not to say 'California here I come!'.

BACKGROUND – A PICTURE OF CALIFORNIA

One of the most obvious things about California is its number of Spanish place names. History answers the question 'Why?', for intrepid Spanish explorers were the first white men to set foot on what was, up to the 16th century, Indian territory. Sebastian Vizcaino, one of these explorers, 'discovered' and named San Diego, Catalina Island, Santa Barbara, Monterey and Carmel in the early 1600s.

Even the state name was borrowed from a Spanish story and was first used in referring to the Pacific coastline in the early 1530s.

It was the Spanish who sent soldiers and priests to create communities and build Missions, and the cattle they brought with them were eventually to bring this land great wealth. Fruit and vines, too, first grown in Mission gardens, were to boost the economy in future years.

Cattle raising became big business after 1822 when Mexico, having won its independence from Spain and being in power over the area now known as California, issued land grants which allowed an individual to own several ranches. Cowboys came into being, as did the rodeo for the rounding up and branding to distinguish which cattle belonged to whom. The ranch owners became rich, took to wearing lots of silver, and were known as the 'Silver Dons'. Land squabbles and bad natural conditions caused the breakup of the enormous ranches in the 1860s, but their dissolution signalled the start of real estate development.

Oranges and Vines

As for those other crops grown first in Mission gardens, oranges brought the biggest success. By 1872 Los Angeles

The first in California's famous chain of Missions was established at San Diego in 1769

BACKGROUND

County boasted 35,000 orange trees and the idea soon spread to neighbouring counties. Industry expansion resulted in a marketing organisation formed by the growers in the 1890s. Its important successor, California Fruit Growers' Exchange, was started in 1905, using the trade name 'Sunkist'. Today when you tour the vine-clad valleys of the Napa and Russian Rivers, sampling the products which have become world famous, you can thank the Spanish, too. The first grape cuttings were laid in San Diego, and soon other Missions were planting vines – the basis of early Californian vineyards. However, it was later immigrants from other countries who developed vine growing into an industry, most notably the Germans, French and Hungarians. By 1879, about 150,000 acres (67,000 hectares) were being used for grapes, and although Californian wine has only been 'recognised' in Europe relatively recently, wineries were widely fashionable in the mid-1880s.

Railroads and Gold

California is a land of immigrants, as you will quickly note while travelling around. They came to seek glory and fortune, to work on the railroad, or merely for a new start in life. If there are numerous Chinese Out West, it's because their numbers were swollen by workers coming to help build the railways in the 1860s and 70s. Today's San Francisco

tourist attraction, Chinatown, back in those times was full of brothels and opium dens. The discovery of gold in 1848 not only brought in foreigners, but also a rush of Americans to the Sierra. Suddenly, the state's population quadrupled, small hamlets became boom towns, and new communities mushroomed in mining areas. After the peak year of 1852, many despondent miners returned to other work in the cities, leaving ghost towns behind them. But some adventurers never even reached the mines, like the 'forty-niners' who were trapped in Death Valley.

Tales of gold drew hordes of hopeful 'forty-niners' to the Sierra. Many went away empty-handed

Funnily enough, California's best-known millionaires didn't strike it rich from gold in that original 'rush', but from a later discovery in the neighbouring state of Nevada known as 'The Comstock Lode'. Men who became wealthy from the rich deposits of gold and silver found there included Adolph Sutro, who became mayor of San Francisco, and James Fair, who created what is now the celebrated Fairmont Hotel. Other men made their fortunes from the railroad and you will find their names perpetuated throughout California. 'The Big Four' – Leland Stanford, Collis Huntington, Mark Hopkins and Charles Crocker – were all ambitious merchants. The first three founded the Central Pacific Railroad and were later joined by Crocker. After the railroad's completion in 1869, they concentrated on the San Francisco Bay region, the central valley and a coastal route.

The Real and Imaginary West

Not surprisingly, transport was a key to the growth of the West, but its stage-coach beginnings are something tourists still associate with California. Who hasn't heard of the Pony Express and one of its famous riders, 'Buffalo Bill' Cody? Who hasn't heard of Wells Fargo, whose wagons often carried gold and were just as often robbed? Who hasn't heard the words 'Throw down the box' (albeit on screen), originally used by highwayman 'Black Bart'? The 'screen' and films are nowadays naturally associated with Hollywood, but actors and actresses came to California long before Hollywood became a household word. After 1870, the state showed a particular interest in culture and attracted many writers and artists. The village of Hollywood itself first began to be noticed when it played host to the film industry during World War I's temporary stoppage of European film-making. By the 1920s, it was *the* movie centre, where matinée idols dripped diamonds, and epic upon epic was produced. The stars built magnificent homes in Beverly Hills and in Los Angeles' beach resorts like Malibu. And they brought glitter to the then tiny desert oasis of Palm Springs.

BACKGROUND

Anza-Borrego Desert – a landscape largely unchanged since California's beginnings

Film stars, though, are not necessarily responsible for the fads and fancies that seem so evident in California. During the first part of the 20th century, hordes of migrants flocked to southern California in search of work. They came from different social and religious backgrounds and brought new ideas which sometimes resulted in cults that would have proved unacceptable elsewhere.

Natural Wonders

Some of the greatest pleasures for visitors are provided by California's natural wonders, which early conservationists helped preserve. One name which springs immediately to mind is John Muir. He not only gave his name to Muir Woods (a National Monument close to San Francisco), but also campaigned vigorously for the protection of Yosemite Valley, the state's first park in 1864. Death Valley, such an obstacle to 19th-century travellers intent on reaching California, is today a National Park and dramatic sightseeing excursion. Giant redwoods and sequoias, while no longer abundant as in Spanish times, have been preserved in special parks, too, and much of Anza-Borrego Desert State Park remains as wild as it was in the days of the pioneers.

Being a coastal state, California's beaches are equally a plus factor. These days, the city of Los Angeles has grown sufficiently to merge with several seaside resorts, referred to as 'The American Riviera'. Malibu, Santa Monica and Newport are favourites. Across the bay from San Francisco, beach-fronted Sausalito has a Mediterranean atmosphere, as does La Jolla in the vicinity of San Diego.

SAN FRANCISCO

San Francisco is, without doubt, a beautiful city. It is built on hills overlooking a bay that is spanned by one of the world's most celebrated bridges – Golden Gate. It is also a sophisticated city which has cultivated the arts ever since the end of the 'pioneer' phase in about 1870 – by the end of the 19th century its opera season was one of America's finest and its symphony orchestra was one of the first to receive regular financial assistance from public funds. But it can also be bawdy – almost as much as during the Gold Rush days when gambling and vice were the norm as befitted a boom town.

Despite being an important banking, insurance and shipping centre, San Francisco is a fun place to be, noted for its cable cars, fine restaurants, colourful waterfront, and the largest Asian community outside of Asia. With less than a million residential population and confined to 47 square miles (122sq km), San Francisco is easy to explore. Its Spanish heritage, charming neighbourhoods and year-round temperate climate (yes, rain and mist, too) add to the magic of the place referred to by John Steinbeck as 'a golden handcuff with the key thrown away'.

Another writer, William Saroyan, insisted 'you can't get bored in San Francisco', perhaps because it never went through the provincial town stage. Once gold was discovered in 1848 in the nearby Sierra foothills, what had been the sleepy settlement of Yerba Buena sprang up almost overnight into an eclectic, heterogeneous hotchpotch of a city. It has never been conventional. Most of the streets slant at an angle, and where else would they build an 'earthquake-proof' skyscraper – the Transamerica Pyramid? Only San Francisco would put a statue of Ben

City lights beckon – nearing San Francisco on the Bay Bridge

SAN FRANCISCO

Franklin (not George) in its Washington Square and suggest that you don't hasten for an ambulance when you hear moans, groans and wails – it's the foghorns.

San Francisco is full of surprises: here a gilded dragon, there a kite flyer or a pavement string quartet. As they say, this is the crossroads to everywhere – served by over 30 steamship lines and more than 50 airlines, and within easy range of the Sierra highspots, Yosemite and Lake Tahoe, the soft-serene Monterey–Carmel Peninsula, giant redwoods and the arty Mendocino coast.

Getting around the city itself is easy, even if not on foot. Riding the metro and buses that operate throughout the MUNI 700-mile (1,100km) system will not break the bank – free transfers are included except on the cable cars. Cabs and car rentals are in ready supply.

The ferry service to Sausalito, Tiburon, Larkspur and the islands in the Bay is inexpensive and efficient. It is also easy to use the 71-mile (114km) Bay Area Rapid Transit (BART) system which links San Francisco with Daly City to the south and the East Bay counties by a 3½ mile (5.6km) underwater tunnel. By car, you can cross the Bay on the city's 'other' bridge, 8½ miles (13.6km) long San Francisco–Oakland Bay Bridge.

Finding something to do is no problem, as besides the sights and the views and the shops and the Paris-style pavement cafés and the restaurants, there are also the sports and events. This is the home of the San Francisco 49er's football team, but there is also baseball, basketball, horse-racing, yachting, fishing and golf.

Chinatown's New Year celebration is a festive occasion, and other highlights include a Cable Car Bell Ringing Contest, film festival, fairs and floral displays.

It is difficult not to fall in love with the place. As Rudyard Kipling so wisely pointed out: 'San Francisco has only one drawback – 'tis hard to leave'.

Cable cars like this have been tackling San Francisco's notorious gradients for more than a century

WHAT TO SEE IN AND AROUND SAN FRANCISCO

A boat trip across the Bay to one of the islands is a 'must'

ALCATRAZ

A visit to Alcatraz is almost irresistible because until 1963 it was America's most secure, and therefore most feared, prison, known as 'The Rock'. No lawbreaker imprisoned here ever escaped *and* lived to tell the tale. Its grim past has made it a popular sightseeing attraction, albeit a chilling one. It is thought to have acquired its name from the Spanish word for pelican, *alcatrace*, a bird said to have inhabited the island in Spanish explorer times. Today you will see the prison exercise yard, empty except for other tourists, with its concrete seats and guard-tower-topped walls. You will be able to take an audio-cassette tour through the main cell

block, listening to narrations by former inmates and guards. Because it is so popular, make a reservation for your tour of Alcatraz (tel: (415) 546 2700). The 12-acre (5-hectare) island lies 1½ miles (2.4km) off the San Francisco shore and is reached by a special ferry boat from Pier 41.

◆
ANGEL ISLAND

This is the largest island in the Bay, taking its name from the Spanish one – Nuestra Senora de los Angeles – given by the commander of the *San Carlos*, the first ship to sail through the Golden Gate. Looking a little like Corsica, it has been used for a variety of purposes, but today is a state park with deer. Its 12 miles (19km) of roads

SAN FRANCISCO

and hiking trails, picnic area and small museum, make it an agreeable destination. Tours leave from the Visitor Center from April to September. The island is reached by ferry from Pier 43½, Tiburon or Vallejo.

◆
BANK OF AMERICA
California St
The focal point of this landmark skyscraper is its formal plaza with an abstract black-granite sculpture designed by Japan's Masayuki Nagare. Locally (and perhaps cynically) the piece is referred to as 'the Banker's Heart'! More important to most tourists is the panoramic restaurant and bar, the Carnelian Room, at the summit of this 52-storey office complex.

◆◆◆
CABLE CAR MUSEUM
Washington and Mason Sts
Cable cars are very special to San Francisco, although these days they only operate on three routes. When their complete disappearance was threatened, private individuals raised millions of dollars, and this, plus money from the state and federal governments, was enough to preserve them. Their control centre (a 1907 red-brick barn sited on the original 1887 foundation of the Ferries and Cliff House Railway Co building) was rebuilt and reopened in 1964 as a municipal showplace. This cable car powerhouse and car barn still contains the operating machinery, but it

Loved by locals and tourists alike, cable cars are preserved

also houses vintage cable cars, including the very first, launched in 1873, plus 57 scale models of types of other cable car, photographs and assorted memorabilia. Forty cable cars are stabled in the barn. During the year they carry some 14 million passengers, a large percentage of them tourists. The cars may only travel at just over 9mph (14kph), but there's no better way to enjoy San Francisco's breathtaking vistas. You pay to ride but a visit to the museum is free.

◆◆
CALIFORNIA ACADEMY OF SCIENCES
Golden Gate Park
A must for anyone with a bent towards the sciences – from

outstanding Steinhart Aquarium where thousands of fresh and salt-water fish are at home. This section also includes an alligator swamp. The true star attraction, though, is the Alexander F Morrison Planetarium, where star shows are given several times daily.

◆◆◆
CALIFORNIA PALACE OF THE LEGION OF HONOR
Lincoln Park
If you have time for only a few museums, this should be one of them. Located on a hilltop, it is a replica of its famous Paris namesake and was given to San Francisco in 1924 by the Spreckels family. It houses an all-French collection of art, including many Rodin bronzes. Open Wednesday to Sunday. Entrance is free on the first Wednesday and Saturday morning of each month. (Closed for expansion until late 1995.)

◆◆◆
CHINATOWN ✓

Grant Ave
Almost a city within a city, San Francisco's Chinatown is the largest settlement of its kind outside Asia. The main artery of this 16-block exotic labyrinth of shops, restaurants and landmarks, is Grant Avenue. Where it intersects Bush Street stands the ornamental, green-tiled gateway that marks the frontier of the Oriental stronghold. The quarter officially ends at Broadway. Chinatown is as congested as any Hong Kong side-street, and best explored on foot. As befits any Oriental quarter,

fossils to space – since the displays in many fascinating halls can be viewed under the one roof. It is the West's oldest science institution – moved to its present location after the big fire of 1906. Recommended for children, entrance to the Academy is free on the first Wednesday of every month. American mammals in natural settings can be found in the Hall of Mammals; similarly, a huge collection of birds are housed in their own hall and geological exhibits are displayed in the Hall of Minerals. In another wing is the Simson African Hall, containing hunting trophies presented to the museum by Leslie Simson, a mining engineer who loved the sport. The latest attraction is Life Through Time, and don't miss the Wattis Hall of Man, nor the

SAN FRANCISCO

there are dragon-entwined lamp-posts and pagoda-topped telephone boxes, not to mention the calligraphy street signs. Many buildings have arched eaves, carved cornices and filigreed balconies. Grocery shops overflow with Chinese delicacies; gift shops are crammed with rare and not so rare art objects and souvenirs; eating places include tea houses that specialise in *dim sum* and some of the best restaurants in town.

The lure of the gold mines and work on the railroad brought numerous Chinese immigrants to San Francisco. The community today is estimated to be as large as 160,000. To find out more about the contributions made by the early Chinese to Californian industries, visit the **Chinese Historical Society** on Commercial Street (open Wednesday to Sunday; free). The **Chinese Culture Center** (open Tuesday to Saturday; free) on Kearny Street features changing exhibitions of Chinese arts and crafts.

If there is one tranquil spot in this bustling and colourful district, it is **St Mary's Square**, dominated by the 12ft (3.6m) statue of Dr Sun Yat-sen, founder of the Republic of China. Diagonally across from

The bright lights of Chinatown, an integral part of city nightlife

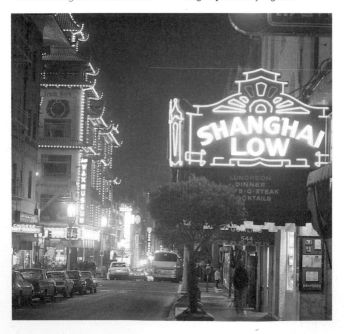

the Square, on the Grant-California corner, is a most un-Chinese edifice – **Old St Mary's Church**. This, California's first cathedral, was largely built by Chinese labourers in 1854 from brick brought around Cape Horn and granite cut in China. Three other more-Oriental religious institutions of note are the **Kong Chow Temple** at Clay and Stockton Streets, the **Tien Hou Temple** on Waverly Place, and **Buddha's Universal Church** on Washington Street.

What looks like a three-tiered 'temple' on Washington Street (and is actually the Bank of Canton) used to house the Chinatown Telephone Exchange. Before 1949 when the dial system took over, the operators here were so proficient in dialects and had such fantastic memories, that they were able to connect hundreds of subscribers who asked for their party by name, not number.

Chinatown is at its most magnificent during festival times: the spring Festival of the Tombs, the summer Dragon Boat Celebration, the autumn Moon Festival, and most especially Chinese New Year.

◆
CIVIC CENTER
Golden Gate Ave
Said by many architects to be the finest civic centre in the United States, this one is graced by a City Hall that boasts a higher dome than Washington's. In addition to the State and Federal Office Buildings, there is the Bill

Dignified and stately – the City Hall

Graham Civic Auditorium which can seat as many as 7,000 people attending one of its sporting or cultural events. Complementing this is the Performing Arts Center and, beneath the Plaza, the Brooks Hall. Nearby is the **Asian Art Museum** (open Wednesday to Sunday) which contains Avery Brundage's vast collection of Oriental art treasures, including some noteworthy jades.

◆◆
COIT TOWER
Lombard St and Telegraph Blvd
This rather improbable structure on top of Telegraph Hill was built in 1934 at the bequest of Lillie Hitchcock Coit, who left $125,000 to the city. Murals depicting

Californian life in the 1930s decorate the Tower's gallery, but the real reason for a visit here is the view. From the 210ft (64m)-high observation platform the panorama of Bay and city spreads before you. The hill on which the tower stands was christened 'Telegraph' in earlier days when a semaphore was used to signal the approach of ships through the Golden Gate.

◆

EMBARCADERO CENTER
Clay St

A highly visible bayside complex, the Embarcadero Center comprises several buildings that house shops, restaurants, offices, hotels and the restored Old Federal Bank.

◆

FERRY BUILDING
Market St

Still very much a San Francisco landmark, the Ferry Building was patterned after the Giralda Tower in Seville. It is headquarters for the Port of San Francisco and the World Trade Center. Before the Bay bridges were built, 50 million ferry-boat commuters a year passed through this bayside entry point. Today, at the terminal's southern end, ferries depart for Sausalito and Larkspur; at the northern end, for Alameda, Oakland, Vellejo and Tiburon.

◆◆◆

FISHERMAN'S WHARF
Bounded by The Embarcadero and Columbus Ave

The most popular (and touristy) district in town! Many people come to this area to eat in the seafood restaurants clustered along the front, facing the brightly painted fishing boats, or by purchasing fresh fish and sourdough bread from the food stalls and bakeries. Queues are especially long when crab is in season (mid-November to May).

Tourists also come to the Wharf to shop, if not from the roadside crafts stalls, most certainly at The Cannery and Ghirardelli Square, both smart complexes converted from factories. They also come to enjoy the street entertainment – there's always something happening in this part of town. In the vicinity, the **Maritime National Historical Park** has a strong appeal to children. Located at the foot of Beach and Polk Streets, it contains many nautical artefacts from Gold Rush days.

The flotilla of historic ships at Hyde Street Pier is also part of the museum. Here, the last ship of the Cape Horn fleet is moored – the square-rigged *Balclutha*, built in Scotland in 1886.

Other treasures include a steam schooner, a side wheel commuter ferry, and river and ocean-going tugs. You may also view the last of World War II's 'Liberty' ships, the SS *Jeremiah O'Brien*, at Pier 3, and board a fleet submarine, the USS *Pampanito*, at Pier 45. Boat excursions of the San Francisco Bay area leave from Piers 39 and 41.

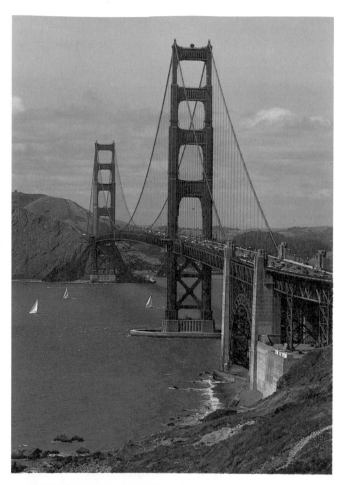

Never golden, but handsome – the Golden Gate Bridge

◆◆◆
GOLDEN GATE BRIDGE ✓

This is one of the world's most famous bridges, although it's not actually golden coloured! Opened in 1937 at a cost of $35 million, it was designed by Joseph Strauss and was, until 1964, the longest, single-span suspension bridge. The best vantage point is Vista Point on the northern approach. The bridge is just north of the city, on Highway 1. There is a toll southbound only. Pedestrians and cyclists cross free.

◆◆◆
GOLDEN GATE PARK
Lincoln Way and Fulton
The place for a little solace, a little recreation, a little band music. Before Scottish landscape gardener John McLaren arrived on the San Francisco scene, what is now such a popular park was nothing but sand dunes. McLaren discovered that there were varieties of shrubs and grass which would hold the sand in place and, thanks to his careful cultivation, today there is a wealth of flowery dells, arboreta and botanical gardens. A statue of the man stands in the dell named for him, where 300 varieties of rhododendrons blossom. Another floral attraction is the **Conservatory of Flowers**, modelled after London's Kew Gardens, where a large and varied collection of tropical flowers is grown. Six thousand plant species, including rare Californian redwoods, give the **Strybing Arboretum** and **Botanical Gardens** their reputation, whilst **Shakespeare's Garden of Flowers** contains all those ever mentioned in the Bard's plays. **The Japanese Tea Garden** is a 5-acre (2-hectare) legacy from the 1894 Midwinter International Exposition. With its shinto shrines, wishing bridge and miniature trees, it looks at its most authentic in spring when the cherry trees bloom.
The park also has a baseball pitch and polo field, a children's playground and Spreckels Lake for model boats. On Stow Lake, the largest of the artificial lakes, rented canoes, rowing boats and motor boats may be taken out. In the open-air auditorium of the Music Concourse, Sunday concerts are given in good weather. Within the park are several museums. The most important are the **California Academy of Sciences** (see pages 14–15) and the **M H de Young Memorial Museum** (see pages 26–7).

◆
GRACE CATHEDRAL
California and Taylor Sts
Charles Crocker once had a mansion on this site. Today, Grace is the country's third largest Episcopal cathedral, and one of the most impressive examples of gothic architecture in the US. Built in 1928, its east entrance is embellished by replicas of the Ghiberti doors of the Florence Baptistry. Admission free.

Grace Cathedral – a detail on the ornate main door

◆
HAIGHT-ASHBURY
Buena Vista Park
This area of town was at its most notorious during the 1960s, when it was a hippie haven. It has since been gentrified, though nowadays there are punks among the yuppies.

◆
JACKSON SQUARE
A renovated and revitalised area whose history goes back to San Francisco's boozy, brawling Gold Rush days. Don't look for a proper square, however, as it is more of a narrow rectangle formed by Jackson, Montgomery, Gold and Sansome Streets – a redeveloped district that these days takes in some of the surrounding streets besides. The city's first bridge was built over a backwater in 1844, on the Jackson–Montgomery corner, making a shortcut to the bayfront. Then there were only a few settlers – 5 years later there were thousands. The area became the city's commercial hub with sturdy buildings that withstood the 1906 earthquake and fire. But the rest of San Francisco had to rebuild, and the Jackson district fell into disrepair. The neighbourhood's renaissance began in 1951 and in 1972 it was proclaimed a 'historic district' with 17 landmark buildings.

Of special interest are numbers: 400 Jackson, partly dating from 1859; 415–431 Jackson, built in 1853 and used by Domingo Ghirardelli for his original chocolate factory; 441 Jackson, built in 1861 on the hulls of two abandoned ships; 458–460 Jackson, first occupied in 1854; 470 Jackson, housing consulates in the 1850s and 60s; and 452 Jackson, built in 1850 using ship masts as interior support columns.

◆◆
JAPANTOWN
Some 12,000 Japanese Americans are estimated to live in San Francisco. They started moving into the district known as the Western Addition in the early 1900s, and it was not long before the area acquired the look of a mini Ginza, with import shops and Japanese restaurants. The focal point for visitors is the **Japan Center**, a 5-acre (2-hectare) site occupied by tempura and sushi bars, tea houses and craft stores, and the Miyako Hotel where you'll find both Japanese and Western-style accommodations. Part of the complex is the Peace Plaza whose main feature is a five-tier pagoda designed by the Japanese architect, Yoshiro Taniguchi, and is setting of the springtime Cherry Blossom Festival.

◆◆◆
LOMBARD STREET
Drive down it for a dazzling view and dizzying experience – Lombard Street, often called 'the world's crookedest', descends Russian Hill in nine hairpin bends on the block between Leavenworth and Hyde. The hill itself derives its name from Russian sailors buried here.

◆◆◆
MISSION DOLORES
16th and Dolores Sts
This is the more familiar name for the Mission of San Francisco de Asis, founded by Father Junipero Serra in 1776, but later constructed in its present adobe style. It took the 'Dolores' name from the nearby lake called by the Spaniards 'Languna de Nuestra Senora de los Dolores'. It was the sixth of 21 Missions established by the Franciscans and its crypts and adjacent graveyard are full of early city history. The Mission is most often reached via the clearly marked 49–Mile Scenic Drive.

◆◆
NOB HILL
As its name suggests, this is a place for the well-heeled, with elegant homes and hotels. The name is a contraction of the Hindu word *nabob*, referring to a person who has acquired great wealth – San Francisco's nobs made their fortunes from gold, silver and the railroad in the mid-1800s. In the years following the discovery of gold, this hill, 376ft (115m) above the waterfront, proved an élitist escape hatch from the rowdiness below. Robert Louis Stevenson described it in 1882 as 'the hill of palaces'. It remains a steep hill, but happily the cable car route installed by the millionaire hillside home owners still operates. Disembark at the California/Powell Street intersection for the best view of the Bay. Unfortunately, the grand wooden villas did not survive the 1906 fire, although the only brick (brownstone) residence built by silver king James Flood, and now the private Pacific Union Club, did.

A retreat for the élite, the Fairmont Hotel stands high above the city on Nob Hill

NORTH BEACH
Columbus Ave to Broadway
This colourful neighbourhood is set in a narrow valley between Telegraph and Russian Hills. It was so named because in the 1860s there was a beach here, though later the land was filled in. The area is known as 'Little Italy' as more than 100,000 of its inhabitants are of Italian descent; there are expresso bars and many other Italian influences. It is also the entertainment belt – jazz, cabaret, strip-tease – with offerings from low grade to high quality.

OLD MINT
5th and Mission Sts
Architecturally speaking, this building is said to be one of the best examples of Federal Classical Revival in the West – but it is the pyramid of gold bars in the circular vault that is the dramatic display. The museum contains Western art. Open Monday to Friday; free.

PACIFIC HEIGHTS
One of the smartest areas of the city, shared by consulates and condominiums and great mansions fronting on parterred gardens. The best place to house browse is along the Broadway bluff between Webster and Lyon Streets, where the Hamlin School and Convent of the Sacred Heart are of architectural interest. Mansions of note include the Spreckels (2080 Washington Street), the Whittier (2090 Jackson Street) and the Bourn (2550 Webster Street).

PALACE OF FINE ARTS
3601 Lyon St
Beautifully restored, this 'palace' was built for the 1915 Panama–Pacific Exposition. Today it contains the **Exploratorium**, a much-acclaimed hands-on science museum where some 650 exhibits may be pushed, pulled, manipulated, etc. Open daily in summer (closed Monday rest of the year). Entrance is free on the first Wednesday of every month and every Wednesday evening.

PORTSMOUTH SQUARE
Portsmouth Square is a small historic park in Chinatown where the American flag was raised in 1846 by Captain John Montgomery who claimed California for the United States. By the time New York Mormon, Sam Brannan, arrived with a colonising force 3 weeks later, California had already been annexed by the United States.

PRESIDIO
Presidio were the military attachment to Missions. This one covers a large area just south of the Golden Gate Bridge. Today it is part of the Golden Gate National Recreation Area (GGNRA). The main historic site is the **Presidio Army Museum** (open Wednesday to Sunday; admission free), the city's oldest adobe building. The Presidio is also the start of an ecology trail.

◆
ST MARY'S CATHEDRAL
*Geary and Gough Sts on
Cathedral Hill*
This eminent church was
completed in 1970 on the
same site as the earlier church
of the Catholic Archdiocese of
San Francisco. Rising to 190ft
(58m), it is a bold piece of
architecture. Open on four
sides to permit panoramic city
views, this modern cathedral
features marble, stained glass,
a magnificent baldachin
suspended above the
sanctuary, and a Ruffatti
organ said to be among the
world's best.

SAN FRANCISCO MUSEUM
OF MODERN ART
Third St at Mission St
This newly built art museum is
one of the finest in the country,
located next to the Moscone
Center, it features a
permanent collection of 20th-
century art. Among the
contemporary artworks on
view here are those by
Picasso, Klee and Pollock.
Closed Mondays, admittance
free on the first Tuesday of
each month.

◆◆
SAN FRANCISCO ZOO
Sloat Blvd
One of the top zoos in America
– a real attraction for children.
Popular sections include
Gorilla World, Primate
Discovery Centre and Koala
Crossing. Among the more
unusual residents are snow
leopards, pygmy hippos and
a white tiger. Two-legged and
four-legged kids get together
in the Children's Zoo. Free on
the first Wednesday of each
month and to under 3s.

SAUSALITO
The temptation to cross San
Francisco Bay to the seaside
community of Sausalito is
rarely resistible. Sausalito
may very easily be reached
by the Golden Gate Bridge or
ferry and its laid-back, Riviera
atmosphere is enjoyed by all
who wander this way (the
view back to San Francisco is
worth the trip alone). Sausalito
is certainly picturesque: its
houses, restaurants and
guesthouses are bright with
flowers and cling to the hillside
in precipitous fashion. It is
cheerful, chic and fashionable
– California's answer to Capri
with al fresco terraces above,
bars, discotheques and
boutiques below. Absolutely
recommended for a day
away from the city, or just for
lunch.

◆◆
SEAL ROCKS
Point Lobos Ave
At the foot of Point Lobos
Avenue, look offshore to these
rocks. Binoculars will bring the
shore birds and frolicking sea-
lions into closer view.
Whatever the time of year,
wildlife can be seen – and
you can even watch the
animals in comfort from Cliff
House restaurant. The original
Cliff House was the home of
Adolph Sutro (who broke the
silver kings' monopoly) – he
created an elaborate resort in
this Sutro Heights area in the
1890s.

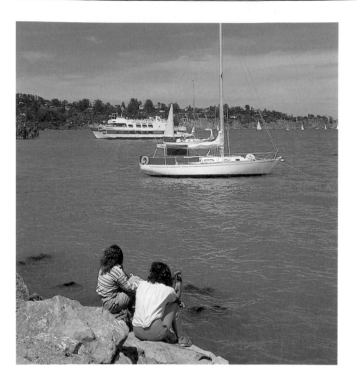

◆◆
SOMA

A 2-square-mile (5 sq km) grid of wide, one-way streets and narrow alleys has been dubbed 'South of Market' (SoMa) and is San Francisco's answer to New York's SoHo. Immigrants and the avant-garde live here; warehouses and workshops have become dance clubs, theatres and restaurants. The area is becoming a mecca for the arts with the $44 million **Center for the Arts at Yerba Buena Gardens** which opened in 1993 and the **San Francisco Museum of Modern Art** (see

That Riviera touch – a view across the Bay from the chic waterside village of Sausalito

page 24) relocating here in 1995. Bargain hunters are attracted by the many factory outlets.

◆◆◆
UNION SQUARE

A hub for shoppers at the heart of the city, Union Square is bordered by department stores and hotels, and filled with strollers and pigeons. The plaque at the Geary–Powell entrance tells you that Mayor John White Geary presented this block to the city for public use as a square in 1850 and that its name derives from the series of violent pro-Union demonstrations held here on the eve of the Civil War. The Victory Monument in the middle of the Square commemorates George Dewey's naval success over the Spanish in Manila in 1898. Dedicated by President Roosevelt in 1903, it survived the subsequent earthquake. The most famous hotel on the Square is the Westin St Francis, dating from 1904 but added to in 1972.

The much newer Grand Hyatt San Francisco on the northeast corner has a plaza featuring a favourite artwork – a fountain sculpted by Ruth Asawa with 41 wraparound bronze friezes that somehow captures the spirit of San Francisco.

If an event is going to take place, more than likely it takes place in Union Square, be it a demonstration or band concert. The most unusual, perhaps, is the annual July Cable Car Bell Ringing Contest.

Above: *The all-American snack*
Right: *Union Square, the heart of fashionable downtown*

◆
VINTAGE HOUSES
Saving Victoriana has become a lifelong project for many San Franciscans, and for those interested, driving routes and walking tours have been designed to take in some of the preserved 'gingerbread'-style houses.

Of particular note is **Octagon House** at Gough and Union Streets, an 1861 heirloom in Cow Hollow (once the city's

dairyland), but it is only open to the public 3 days a month so check for times. The Queen Anne-style **Haas-Lilienthal House** on Franklin Street dates from 1886 and is the only fully furnished Victorian house open to the public (open Wednesdays and Sundays). The **California Historical Society** headquarters, housed in the handsome 1896 brownstone building on Jackson Street, contains a museum and reference library. Open Tuesday to Sunday, free the first Wednesday of each month.

◆◆
M H DE YOUNG MEMORIAL MUSEUM
Golden Gate Park
This, the city's most diversified art museum, has a wealth of masterpieces that include Rubens' *Tribute*

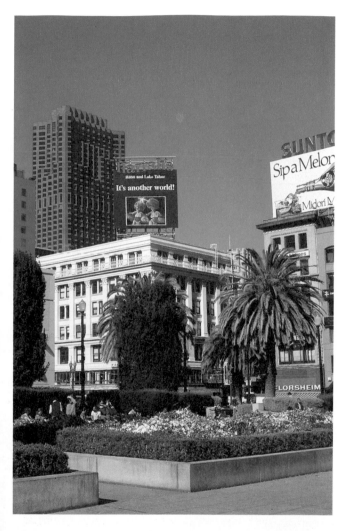

Money and El Greco's *St John the Baptist*. A range of galleries illustrates Western culture from the era of Ancient Greece to the present time, and a large American wing shows off a comprehensive collection of US art. Open Wednesday to Sunday. Free on the first Wednesday of each month, and on Saturday mornings.

SAN FRANCISCO

0   1   2 km

● Bay Area Rapid Transit (BART) Stations
— 49 Mile Scenic Drive

GOLDEN GATE BRIDGE

■ Fort Point
■ National Historic Site

Crissy Field
Golden Gate Promenade
MARINA BLVD

Palace of
Fine Arts ■

PRESIDIO   Presidio
Army
Museum

Baker Beach

Golden Gate
National Recreation Area

South Bay

Lands End

China Beach

PRESIDIO HEIGHT

Lincoln Park

San Francisco Fire Department
Pioneer Memorial Museum ■

Palace of the ■   ● Holocaust
Legion of Honor   Memorial

SEACLIFF

Point
Lobos

■ Veterans Hospital □

POINT   LOBOS   AVE

25TH

CLEMENT   STREET

GEARY   BOULEVARD

ARGUELLO   BLVD

TURK   ST

Seal
Rocks

■ Cliff House

RICHMOND

University of ■
San Francisco

MASONO   AVE

Ocean
Beach

□ FULTON STREET □

M H de
Young
Museum ■

Conservatory
of Flowers Panhandle

Golden Gate Park

*Stow
Lake*

Japanese
Tea Garden

California
● Academy
of Sciences

HAIGHT
ASHBUR

STANYAN   STREET

Strybing Arboretum
& Botanical Gardens

PARNASSUS AVE

LINCOLN WAY

JUDAH   STREET

7TH   AVENUE

BUENA
VISTA

GREAT   HIGHWAY

SUNSET

SUNSET   BOULEVARD

ORTEGA   STREET

1

19TH   AVENUE

Twin
Peaks ■

*Sunset
Reservoir*

FOREST
HILL

TARAVAL   STREET □

DIAMON
Gle

PARKSIDE

PORTOLA   DRIVE

Mt Davidson
▲ 282m

Pine Lake Park   ■ Sigmund
SLOAT   Stern Grove

35

BOULEVARD

ST FRANCIS
WOOD

San Francisco ■
Zoological Gardens

Stonestown
Shopping Center

GLEN PARK

City College of
San Francisco ■

OCEAN   AVENUE

SOUTHERN   FREEWAY

Balbo
Park

*Harding
Park*

LAKE   MERCED   BLVD

■ San Francisco
State University

INGLESIDE

Balbo
Park

*Lake
Merced*

JOHN MUIR DRIVE

Golden Gate
National
Recreation Area

35

BROTHERHOOD   WAY

OCEAN
VIEW

SKYLINE   BOULEVARD

1

280

San Francisc

- - - - -

DALY CITY
● Daly City

29

SAN FRANCISCO

Accommodation

There are more than 29,000 guest rooms in San Francisco. The range includes the super-plush, established hotels, newer, smaller, so-called 'boutique hotels' and a recent surge of neighbourhood bed and breakfast accommodation. Three new hotels have recently opened their doors: the 158-room Mandarin Oriental (which occupies the first two and top eleven floors of the 48-storey First Interstate Center office tower in the Financial District), the 348-room Pan Pacific on Post Street near Union Square (which is affiliated with Hong Kong's Peninsula Group), and Japan Air Lines' 522-room, 25-storey Hotel Nikko at Mason and O'Farrell Streets.

Even newer are the 360-room Park Hyatt on Clay and Battery Streets, Financial District, and the 1,500-room San Francisco Marriott, a block from the Moscone Convention Center on Fourth Street.

There is so much fine accommodation in the city that it is almost a disservice to list any at all, but favourites are:

Fairmont Hotel & Tower, 950 Mason St (tel: (415) 772 5000). A Nob Hill landmark with a supper club that has top-name entertainers. The original building was supposed to be a home for successful businessman, James Fair, but he died before the mansion was completed in 1894. Today, this top-drawer 596-room hotel boasts restaurants, a coffee shop, ten lounges, a shopping arcade and a health club.

The Mark Hopkins Inter-Continental, 1 Nob Hill (tel: (415) 392 3434). Named and originally built for a prominent railroad baron, the Mark Hopkins is a splendid Nob Hill landmark. Today's 390-room hotel is home of the legendary 'Top of the Mark' cocktail lounge, first opened in 1939, from where a panoramic view of the city is possible.

Mandarin Oriental, 222 Sansome St (tel: (415) 885 0999). This sophisticated, 158-room hotel occupies the top eleven floors of the First Interstate Center in the Financial District so the views are excellent. Designed to please discriminating travellers, the Mandarin concentrates on service.

Sheraton Palace, 2 New Montgomery St (tel: (415) 392 8600). This was America's first truly luxury hotel – hosting Generals like Sheridan, Sherman and Grant. Today, as then, its crown jewel is the Garden Court, where marble columns support a glass roof, lit by chandeliers. Now reopened after an 18-month, multi-million-dollar facelift that included upgrading all 550 rooms, this hotel these days features additional meeting space.

Westin St Francis, 335 Powell St (tel: (415) 397 7000). Recent renovations have made this 1,200-room Union Square landmark one of the city's finest hotels. Built in 1904, it is the second oldest hotel and the grand lobby has become a traditional meeting place for visitors. The location on Union Square by the Powell Street cable car line is ideal for serious shopping excursions as well as sightseeing.

Recommended inns include:
The Grove Inn, 890 Grove St (tel: (415) 929 0780). In Alamo Square, this is a turn-of-the-century Victorian-styled 19-room bed and breakfast establishment.

The Queen Anne, 1590 Sutter St (tel: (415) 441 2828). This 1890 building was designed to be a girls' boarding school. It is now a 49-room inn offering complimentary sherry and concierge service. Rates include breakfast and afternoon tea.

Washington Square Inn, 1660 Stockton St (tel: (415) 981 4220). A stylishly remodelled 15-room house – rooms 7 and 8 overlook the square. Breakfast promises fresh orange juice and fresh flowers along with the croissants and coffee. Afternoon tea is also provided.

Restaurants

There are 4,000 to choose from

A modern backdrop for resplendent Victorian 'Painted Ladies'

of many ethnic types and all price brackets. Some favourites are:

Buena Vista, 2765 Hyde St (tel: (415) 474 5044) – a Wharf rendezvous spot that hasn't changed its looks much from the 1800s. It became a legend a couple of decades ago for the introduction of Irish coffee. Bountiful breakfasts are served here, too. Not expensive.

Carnelian Room, Bank of America Building, 555 California St (tel: (415) 433 7500) – room with a view, and what a view! Cocktails and dinner only except for Sunday brunches.

Fior d'Italia, 601 Union St (tel: (415) 986 1886) – the city's oldest Italian restaurant, Fior d'Italia has always kept the minestrone flowing. There is a 'Godfather' room and a 'Tony Bennett' room.

Fleur de Lys, 777 Sutter St (tel: (415) 673 7779). Without a doubt this is the most romantic restaurant in the city and as a bonus, the food is sublime. Chef Hubert Keller prepares classic French cuisine that is without equal. Expensive but worth every cent.

La Folie, 2316 Polk St (tel: (415) 776 5577). The exceptional French cuisine is always memorable at this small, informal restaurant thanks to the mastery of chef Roland Passot. The high prices are justified by the outstanding preparations and presentations. Reservations are a necessity.

Mama's of San Francisco, 398 Geary St (tel: (415) 788 1004) – theatre district eatery where you can indulge in pancakes topped with berries, omelettes filled with green chilli and sour cream, fresh mushrooms or chicken livers, salads and sandwiches.

Postrio, 545 Post St (tel: (415) 776 7825). Celebrity chef Wolfgang Puck created this big, noisy, fun restaurant and manages to serve consistently excellent dishes representing the best of Californian cuisine. People watching can be as impressive as the food and reservations can be impossibly difficult to make.

Samui Thai Cuisine, 2414 Lombard St (tel: (415) 563 4405). Great, inexpensive Thai food within easy walking distance of many motels. Only atmosphere is missing.

Sears' Fine Food, 439 Powell St (tel: (415) 986 1160). The queues out of the door indicate the popularity of this legendary breakfast café. Try the dollar-sized pancakes and waffles.

Shopping

From street stalls where artisans sell their own work to major American department stores like Saks and Macy's, San Francisco has it all. Two of the more interesting department stores are Neiman-Marcus (whose prize feature is its City of Paris dome which city preservationists fought so hard to keep, and won) and the Emporium on Market Street (which also has a grand dome under which one of the world's tallest indoor Christmas trees is suspended each year). Don't miss the San Francisco Shopping Center at Market and Fifth Streets, a vertical mall that made retailing history when it opened in 1988 with its 'store-in-the-sky' on the top five floors and six spiral escalators. Goods may be purchased within a four-block radius of Union Square at the hub of the city, but many other shops are housed in complexes. The major ones are:

The Anchorage, Fisherman's Wharf – a nautical-looking complex within walking distance of both cable cars and cab stands, with Bay viewing points from its decks and outdoor promenades. An array of apparel, leather, jewellery, craft and gift boutiques, art galleries, snack bars and restaurants are all located here.

The Cannery, 2801 Leavenworth St – once Del

In San Francisco the lighter side of life is never far away

Monte's cannery overlooking San Francisco Bay, this is now a three-storey complex of more than 50 chic shops, galleries, restaurants and cafés. Look for gourmet foods, rare wines, fine handicrafts and designer fashions and home furnishings. Street entertainers perform daily in the courtyard.

Crocker Galleria, near Union Square – modelled after Milan's vast Galleria Vittorio Emmanuelle, this tri-level glass-domed pavilion encompasses over 40 shops and restaurants.

Embarcadero Center, between Sacramento and Clay Streets – takes the site of the old waterfront produce market. It is now a complex of 175 shops and restaurants selling just about everything.

There is frequent impromptu entertainment.

Ghirardelli Square, near Fisherman's Wharf – for many years a chocolate factory and now a favourite shopping complex with 70 shops and award-winning restaurants. It was the country's first manufacturing complex to be preserved and cleverly renovated into a retail centre. Some of the original chocolate vats and ovens are still in operation on the plaza level of the Clock Tower. It offers free entertainment.

Japan Center, bounded by Laguna, Geary, Fillmore and Sutter Streets – a 5-acre (2-hectare) complex of restaurants, sushi bars, art galleries, bookstores and Oriental gift shops.

Pier 39 on the waterfront, near Fisherman's Wharf – an abandoned cargo pier which has been transformed into a covered market-place with two levels of restaurants and unique shops plus a marina and waterfront park. Good views, and good entertainment at the family amusement area and the San Francisco Experience theater.

Children

(see also **What to See**)
San Francisco attractions of especial interest to the younger age group include the USS *Pampanito*, a 312ft (95m) submarine on display (with commentary about her war exploits) at Pier 45. They may also well enjoy clambering about the SS *Balclutha*, part of the Maritime National Historical Park at Hyde Street Pier.
The Zoo is a must – it's a great one! And it's free for those under 3. Its newest attractions are the Primate Discovery Center, Koala Crossing and Gorilla World and there's a Children's Zoo.

Across from the Cannery at the Wharf, there is the American Carousel Museum (open for special events only). The International Toy Museum in the Cannery has play areas with Lego and construction sets, and Ripley's Believe It or Not! on Jefferson Street has a host of astounding objects including an actual shrunken human torso and a cable car made of 275,000 matchsticks. Depending upon their ages and inclinations, there are many city museums to appeal to children, but a visit to the Tactile Dome at the Exploratorium (in the Palace of Fine Arts) is a must. So is the California Academy of Sciences for any child fascinated by snakes, dinosaurs and such like. As for family theme parks, the most noteworthy nearby are Marine World Africa USA in Vallejo, 30 miles (48km) to the northeast, and Paramount's Great America in Santa Clara, 45 miles (72km) south.

Watch the world go by on popular Pier 39

Los Angeles. Two centuries ago this was a tiny pueblo

LOS ANGELES

Where does it start, where does it end? This is the perennial question asked by anyone visiting the urban sprawl of the 'City of the Angels' with its spaghetti network of highways and its municipalities which have burst so much at the seams that they've merged. Los Angeles (or LA as it is commonly known) is a county covering over 4,000 square miles (10,300 sq km); it is also a metropolis with a population of 8.8 million people of which 3.4 million live in the city of Los Angeles. The tiny pueblo of 1781 has boomed and bloomed. Today it is a huge world trade centre; a convention city whose Wilshire Boulevard stretches all the way to Santa Monica. It is almost as difficult to locate downtown Los Angeles, because of its many residential and business pockets – Hollywood, Beverly Hills and Marina del Rey, to name but a few – but it is easy to find where it all began, on Olvera Street. Some people would say that the central point of LA is Hollywood Boulevard where it crosses Vine – a famous corner that has been crossed by innumerable stars. Film stars have helped make LA legendary, living in Bel Air homes, patronising Rodeo Drive shops. They have created new centres for screen activity, such as Universal City and Burbank, and added a magic to doorstep beach resorts like Malibu. The city's elasticity means that it meets the Pacific at such settlements. Wheels are practically an essential – cars are kings in

LOS ANGELES

Los Angeles. (Indeed, it was 'black gold' – petroleum – which proved so profitable for the city early this century.) Those who don't choose to meet the challenge of driving here can, of course, take organised excursions to places of interest, but should give some thought to their accommodation base. Downtown, for example, is crammed during the daytime, both with commuters and cars, but is likely to be deserted at night. Finding a taxi on the street is difficult so you are recommended to call for one or use the central city shuttle minibus (DASH) which operates a frequent service between points of interest every 5 to 20 minutes for just 25 cents. The downtown area is considered to incorporate everything around the Civic Center, the business and financial district, and Commercial and Exposition Parks.

Often 'pockets' are cities in their own right, like West Hollywood (Greater Los Angeles' 84th city), which covers part of the flatland section of Hollywood. The latter's hilly section spans places like Nichols and Laurel Canyons. Once a camping ground for the Cahuenga Indians, Hollywood later became a main stop for the Butterfield Stage and was made a city in 1903. Beverly Hills is also a city, designed for the Rodeo Land and Water Company in 1907; Westwood, another.

With mountains, beaches, valleys and a desert to its credit, Los Angeles can justifiably boast it has something for everyone. Wherever your base, you won't be short of accommodation, shops or nightlife.

Song-famed MacArthur Park

WHAT TO SEE IN AND AROUND LOS ANGELES

◆◆◆
BEVERLY HILLS

Everyone must have heard of Beverly Hills, where the stars come and go. Organised bus tours take tourists around the stars' homes, pointing out the most famous, though these days many a doctor and lawyer reside in the splendid mansions, as well as the screen celebrities.

The district was originally sheep farms and bean fields. In the late 19th century, it was drilled for oil without success, but in 1900 the Amalgamated Oil Company discovered something just as valuable – water – at Rancho Rodeo de las Aguas (ranch of the gathering of the waters). Hence, company president, Burton Green, planned an exclusive residential community for the site to be called Beverly Hills.

The new development only took off once the Beverly Hills Hotel had been built and began attracting the movie moguls and their entourages. When the Polo Lounge was added in the 1930s, prestige rose even more.

The heart of the community is Rodeo Drive, named for the original Rancho – a premier shopping street for designer label seekers, and star spotters.

Adjoining Beverly Hills is another exclusive community, Bel Air, whose wealthy mansions and estates may just about be glimpsed

Famous hideaway for famous people

behind their secure gates and walls.

◆
CHINATOWN
N Broadway

This is a quarter to see on foot. It is a typically Oriental sector where you'll find Chinese grocery and gift shops plus restaurants that specialise in Cantonese and Szechuan cuisine.

◆
DESCANSO GARDENS
Descanso Drive, La Canada Flintridge

These gardens are particularly famous for their camellias – 100,000 of them in an oak forest setting. Descanso also features extensive rose gardens, a Japanese garden, lake, bird sanctuary, art gallery, tea house, and a picnic area. For a small entrance fee, visitors may walk around at leisure or take a tram tour (additional charge).

EXPOSITION PARK
Figueroa St at Exposition Blvd
A 114-acre (46-hectare) park containing the University of California, some of the city's major museums, a 17,000 bush rose garden, the 92,000 seater Los Angeles Memorial Coliseum, and the 16,000 seat indoor Sports Arena.

The **California Museum of Science and Industry**, here, is an impressive hands-on museum which allows learning to be fun. Subjects explained in surprising ways include electricity, internal combustion and communications.

There are also exhibits on health and the human body, and aerospace. Free except the IMAX Theater.

In the **Los Angeles County Natural History Museum**, major halls are devoted to minerals, palaeontology, living mammals, insects and birds, but there is also a section which relates to Californian history between 1540 and 1940. Closed Monday, free on the first Tuesday of each month.

FARMERS MARKET
Fairfax and Third Sts
During the Depression 18 farmers were allowed to set up stalls here, rent free, to sell their produce directly to the public. Today, there are over 110 shops in what has become a city landmark, and you can buy fresh food or sample it at take-away kiosks or sit-down cafés. The range is a wide one, from doughnuts to oyster bars, and prices are affordable.

FOREST LAWN MEMORIAL-PARK
Glendale
This amazing cemetery, more then 300 acres (120 hectares) of lawns and garden retreats, inspired Evelyn Waugh's satire, *The Loved One*, which used the fictitious name 'Whispering Glades'. The highlight is the Great Mausoleum, which houses a number of deceased celebrities including Clark Gable and Jean Harlow. At the Memorial Court of Honor, here, the 'Last Supper' stained-glass window is based on Leonardo da Vinci's famous painting. It is the work of Rosa Moretti, who is said to have had a secret process for making stained glass.

In a special theatre next to the Forest Lawn Museum (where Ghiberti's Paradise Doors have been reproduced), a curtain goes up every half hour to reveal one of the largest paintings on canvas, Jan Styka's *The Crucifixion*.

Throughout Forest Lawn there are replicas of renowned statuary, most notably Michelangelo's *David* in the Court of David. Among the churches within the grounds are ones whose designs are based on 10th-century English and 14th-century Scottish examples. Free.

◆◆◆
GRAUMAN'S CHINESE THEATER
Hollywood Blvd

This prime Hollywood tourist attraction, now called simply Mann's Chinese Theater, was opened in 1927 by showman Sid Grauman who imported Oriental pillars for it. Whenever a film was premiered here, at what was billed the 'King of Theaters', stars were invited to make their hand or foot imprint in the cement forecourt. Some decided to be more original and made good use of their trademarks – Betty Grable, for example, left an imprint of her leg; Gene Autry, the hoofprints of his beloved horse – imprints date from 1927 to present day.

Grauman's first theatre was actually *The Egyptian* across the way, built in 1922, and designed as an ancient palace of Thebes. In its heyday, it was the setting for many glamorous movie premieres. Free, but a film charge.

◆◆
GRIFFITH PARK
North end of Vermont Ave

Occupying over 4,000 acres (1,600 hectares) in the hills above the city, this park is a favourite recreational area. Once part of the Rancho Los Feliz land grant, it is named

Gaze at the heavens from the Griffith Observatory in Griffith Park, on Mount Hollywood

after the Welsh newspaperman, Griffith J Griffith, who donated it to Los Angeles in 1896. Its natural mountainside greenery is perfect for picnics and sports like horseback riding and hiking. One of the prettiest areas is Ferndell, planted with ferns from around the world. Within the park there are several sites of interest, some, like **Travel Town** (free) with its collection of railway locos, and the **Los Angeles Zoo**, are recommended for children. **The Gene Autry Western Heritage Museum** displays cowboy memorabilia from a century of Western films along with historic cowboy artefacts. Summer performances are given by top entertainers in the **Greek Theatre**, a leading amphitheatre, but the park 'highlight' is the **Griffith Observatory**, a copper-domed structure on top of Mount Hollywood. In its theatre you can easily take a trip to the stars or see a laserium show, whilst from the twin refracting telescope in the Hall of Science, you can take a peek at the heavens on a clear night. Closed Mondays in winter. Free except for the planetarium.

◆◆
HANCOCK PARK
Wilshire Blvd
In recreational terms this is a modest park, but Hancock does contain some major museums, including the **Los Angeles County Museum of Art**, which was designed by William Pereira as three pavilions. Most of the permanent collections are

in the central Ahmanson Gallery where you will find numerous Impressionist paintings, American art, selections from the Armand Hammer collection of Roman glass and a much-prized collection of Indian and Islamic art pieces. Changing exhibitions are presented in the Frances and Armand Hammer wing; concerts, lectures and films in the Bing Theater wing. The recent addition to the museum, the Robert O Anderson Building, contains many contemporary paintings including those by Matisse, Picasso and Braque. In the sculpture garden, works on view include those by Moore, Calder and Rodin. Closed Mondays. Free admission on the second Wednesday of each month.

The **George C Page Museum** houses the fossils recovered from the adjacent La Brea Tar Pits, the largest Pleistocene collection ever found in a single location. More than a million fossils have been gathered, including those of mastodons, giant vultures and sabre-toothed tigers – even the remains of an Ice Age woman. Closed Mondays. Free admission on the first Tuesday of each month.

◆
HERITAGE SQUARE
Homer St
A 10-acre (4-hectare) park where Victorian structures from other neighbourhoods have been brought and restored. Its principal sites (all dating from about 1887) are the Hale House, Palms Depot and

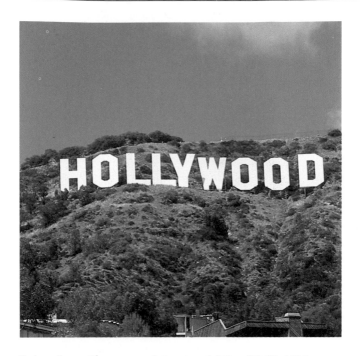

Perhaps the most famous name in America – in letters 50ft (15m) high

Shaw House. Open weekends and holidays.

◆◆◆
HOLLYWOOD ✓

These days, it is difficult to define the boundaries of Hollywood, but one thing is for sure, its **Walk of Fame** (both sides of Hollywood Boulevard from Gower to Sycamore, and both sides of Vine Street from Yucca to Sunset) must have seen more feet than practically anywhere else. The 'Walk' encompasses 5 acres (2 hectares) of bronze stars set into the pavement as a lasting tribute to those who helped make Hollywood great.

It was at Sunset Boulevard and Gower Street that films were first made in earnest in 1911, and in a few years there was a host of warehouse-style studios and a bustling industry. Today, the Hollywood glow is not as rosy, though the Paramount and Goldwyn studios still have their headquarters here, and the famed 'Hollywood' sign (on the slopes of Mount Lee in the Hollywood Hills) continues to shine. As a point of trivia, that 50ft (15m) sign was originally designed to advertise a real estate development when it

The **Queen Mary**, *flanked by the Catalina ferry and the geodesic dome*

read 'Hollywoodland'.
Also in the hills is the
Hollywood Bowl, Frank Lloyd Wright's magnificent amphitheatre. This is the summer home of Los Angeles Philharmonic, which gives classical and pop concerts here. Other performers present jazz, rock, country and folk. A museum of the history of the Bowl is here too.
To the south of the Bowl, the **Hollywood Studio Museum** (open weekends) is housed in the barn used by Cecil B De Mille for the making of the film *The Squaw Man*, and declared a state monument in the 1950s.
In the **Hollywood Wax Museum**, on Hollywood Boulevard, anyone who was – or is – anyone in pictures is represented. The museum features its own film theatre where past Academy Award winners may be viewed, and its own Chamber of Horrors

with scenes and props from famous chillers.
Hollywood Memorial Park, on Santa Monica Boulevard, is the last resting place of old-time greats like Tyrone Power, Rudolph Valentino and Cecil B De Mille.

LITTLE TOKYO
San Pedro and First Sts
The city's Japanese quarter sells and serves, as one might expect, everything Japanese. The focal point of Little Tokyo is the Japanese Village Plaza – an outdoor shopping and dining mall.

LONG BEACH
A city doorstep beach community, this area has

recently been revitalised enough to become of considerable tourist interest. It boasts several museums, entertainment facilities and shopping complexes, and every April hosts the Toyota Grand Prix.

Of especial interest is the *Queen Mary*, one of the largest passenger ships ever built, and now moored in the harbour at the southern end of Long Beach Freeway and operating as a hotel and entertainment/shopping/musem complex. The southern section of Long Beach, known as Naples, is famous for the canals that meander past an eclectic mixture of restored residential architecture. Most of the street names are Italian, so not surprisingly, gondolas are a common sight and the ideal way to tour the area. Even hearing an Italian aria echoing across the water is not unusual.

◆
LOS ANGELES ARBORETUM
310 N Baldwin Ave, Arcadia
This 127-acre (51-hectare) estate features plants from around the world, and its begonias and orchids are particularly noteworthy. Shops and eating facilities can be found on the premises, and another attraction is the ornate Queen Anne cottage, once the home of the property's former owner, silver miner and rancher, Elias Jackson (Lucky) Baldwin. Free on the third Tuesday of each month.

◆
MARINA DEL REY
This beach and watersports centre, with good seafood

restaurants and enticing shops, is within easy access of downtown LA. A number of hotels and motels are conveniently situated around the large marina which is located between the international airport and the resort of Santa Monica. Harbour cruises are available.

◆◆
MISSIONS
Two Christian Missions survive in the Greater Los Angeles area. **San Fernando Rey de Espana**, in Mission Hills, was founded by Fermin Francisco de Lasuon in 1797. Since being restored, it displays many fine examples of Indian and Spanish architecture and is set in 7 acres (3 hectares) of grounds. **San Gabriel Arcangel** was started by the great founder of California's Missions, Father Junipero Serra, in 1771. The church, which dates from 1805, is famous for its bells, and the museum illustrates early Mission life. San Gabriel Arcangel is at 15151 San Fernando Mission Boulevard.

◆
MUSIC CENTER
1st St and Grand Ave
For those who enjoy the performing arts, this three-theatre complex is one of the best in town. A resident opera company and philharmonic orchestra are the mainstays of the Dorothy Chandler Pavilion, which also hosts other symphonies, operas, ballets and large musical productions. Plays and smaller musicals are staged in the

Ahmanson Theatre and the
Mark Taper Forum.

◆◆

NBC STUDIO
*3000 W Alameda Ave,
Burbank*

The only television studio in
California to offer public
tours. For a small fee you can
find out more about sound,
lighting and special effects,
see behind the scenes, and
view yourself on camera.
NBC is to be found in
Burbank at the inner end of
the San Fernando Valley.

◆◆◆

OLD TOWN

If you care to see where Los
Angeles began, take
yourself to what is now **EL
Pueblo de Los Angeles State
Historic Park** in the heart of
downtown. It was here that 11
families came from Mexico in
1781 to found the city. The best
way to tour is on foot from
Olvera Street, the city's oldest –
a pedestrianised, block-long
Mexican market-place lined
with craft shops and cafés. A
look inside the oldest adobe
house, Avila Adobe, is free, as
is entry to the city's oldest
church fronting the Old Plaza.
Pico House (1870) is almost as
old and was named for
California's last Mexican
governor. It was originally
designed to be a prestigious
three-storey hotel, and you'll
find it on Olvera Street. The
tunnels which led from
warehouses to Pico House
were once gambling and
opium dens.

In the same district, take a
look at the Merced Theater,
the Sepulveda House and the
Pelanconi House and, after the
tour, stroll eastwards to Union
Station, built in 1939 with a

The Ahmanson Theatre – one of three auditoriums at the Music Center

touch of art deco, and still in operation. Free tours available.

PASADENA
This green and pleasant separate city in the San Gabriel Valley does, in fact, come under the umbrella of Los Angeles and is only 11 miles (18km) from downtown. Founded in 1886 and favoured as a winter resort, it is best loved today for its Tournament of Roses Parade and annual Rose Bowl Game. Memorabilia from these events are to be seen in **Tournament House** and **Wrigley Gardens** (free), built by chewing gum magnate, William Wrigley Jr. Two important art museums which should not be missed are the **Norton Simon Museum of Art** and the **Huntington**. The former has both 20th-century works and works from the early Renaissance period. A star attraction is a room full of pictures by Degas, Rembrandt and Renoir. Another of the museum's strong points is its collection of sculptures from India and the Far East. Open Thursday to Sunday. Several British masterpieces, including Gainsborough paintings, as well as numerous 18th and 19th-century European works have found their way to the **Huntington Library, Art Collections and Botanical Gardens**. The 207-acre (84-hectare) estate used to belong to railway tycoon, Henry Huntington, whose former residence is now the art gallery. Other treasures are to be found in the library –

first edition books and manuscripts that include a copy of Chaucer's *Canterbury Tales*.

RESORTS
Anyone who likes to combine their city sights with sun and sand, has their choice of oceanside resorts fringing the Pacific, not far from LA. **Hermosa Beach** and **Manhattan Beach** are among the lesser known, while **Redondo Beach**, established by Henry Huntington, is a somewhat industrialised beach resort that offers good fishing. **Venice** (which never did achieve the developer's plan of looking like Italy's same-name attraction) is a place for people-watching.
The two resorts are Malibu and Santa Monica. **Malibu** found itself a jetset point on the map in the 1920s when the film stars moved here. Even now there is the slight chance of seeing a celebrity face, but, beach and surfing apart, the main Malibu attraction is the **J Paul Getty Museum** on the bluffs above the resort, without doubt one of the world's richest museums, taking up 10 acres (4 hectares) of the 65-acre (26-hectare) Getty estate sometimes sarcastically nicknamed 'Pompeii by the Sea'. The building resembles a Roman villa and is filled with prime Roman and Greek antiquities. There are many exceptional paintings, tapestries and 18th-century French furniture. Closed Mondays. Free.
Santa Monica is a most popular

The J Paul Getty Museum, one of the world's richest, in a latter-day 'Roman villa' above Malibu

beach centre with wonderful white sand, a range of accommodation in all price brackets, interesting restaurants and direct freeway access from downtown LA. It was already an important city in the 1860s, and was adopted as a favoured resort by the 1870s. Like Malibu, it attracted the stars of the 1930s, some of whose palatial homes still stand. Its major landmark is the (now restored) 1909 pier with its turn-of-the-century carousel,

old-fashioned arcade and bumper cars. To the north, along Sunset Boulevard, is the **Will Rogers State Historic Park**, one-time ranch and home of the 1930s humorous cowboy star of that name. Memorabilia and films of his life can be seen in the visitor center, and the 137-acre (55-hectare) grounds incorporate trails, stables, corrals, and picnic areas.

◆◆
SIX FLAGS MAGIC MOUNTAIN
Magic Mountain Parkway, Valencia
A must for children! This theme

park in Valencia may be reached in less than half an hour's drive along the Golden State Freeway from Hollywood. The emphasis is on thrill rides, from log flumes to roller-coasters that loop the loop, though there are gentler amusements for the very young, including a mini zoo and Wizard's Village. One admission price pays for all (children under 4 feet (1.2m) half price), including puppet shows, dance revues and other live entertainment. Open daily from Memorial Day to Labor Day, weekends and holidays only rest of year.

◆◆
SOUTHWEST MUSEUM
234 Museum Drive at Marmion Way, Highland Park
This museum is highly regarded for its expertly researched collection of American Indian relics. Displays cover the Anasazi from the southwest, the Plains Indians, and those from Mexico and Alaska. Museum founder, Charles Lummis (director of the Los Angeles library in 1907) also donated rare books. Closed Mondays.

◆◆◆
UNIVERSAL STUDIOS HOLLYWOOD ✓

100 Universal City Plaza
A fun tour on a candy-coloured tram takes visitors through Universal's 420-acre (170-hectare) studio lot in Universal City. Regulars along the way include an encounter with 'Jaws', a bridge that tumbles underneath the tram, a flash flood and an alpine avalanche. The latest 'thrill' is an earthquake which

collapses the earth under the tram, fells telephone poles, sparks power cables and crashes a runaway propane truck. Also look for 'King Kong', 'The Flintstones Show', 'An American Tail Show', 'Fievels's Playland', 'The Riot Act', 'Back to the Future – The Ride', as well as the 'E.T. Adventure' and the Studio Plaza with shops, shows and restaurants.

◆
WAYFARERS' CHAPEL
Palos Verdes Drive
This glass church was designed by the son of the eminent architect Frank Lloyd Wright, and was erected in 1046 in tribute to the 18th-century Swedish theologian Emanuel Swedenborg. Free.

◆
WELLS FARGO HISTORY MUSEUM
333 S Grand Ave
A recently opened museum showing artefacts, lithographs, photographs and documents about the Old West as they relate to Wells Fargo express and banking company. Closed weekends. Free.

◆
WILLIAM S HART PARK
Newhall Ave
William Hart is considered the prototype of all Western heroes. He willed his ranch and home to the people of Los Angeles. The museum (closed Mondays and Tuesdays) in the old Hart mansion, within the 265-acre (107-hectare) park, contains mementoes of the actor's career as well as Old West relics. The park features a herd of buffalo and picnic sites.

LOS ANGELES

Mission San Fernando
Rey de España

Six Flags Magic Mountain &
William S Hart Park

Verdugo Mountains

210

2 Descanso
Gardens

VAN
NUYS

NORTH
HOLLYWOOD

BURBANK

San Fernando Valley

GOLDEN STATE FREEWAY

5

VENTURA FREEWAY

101

NBC Studios

134

Gene Autry Western
Heritage Museum

Norton Simon
Museum of Art

SHERMAN
OAKS

Universal Studios
Hollywood

Forest
Lawn
Memorial
Park

Griffith
Park

La Zoo

Planetarium

GLENDALE

PASADENA FREEWAY

110

SAN DIEGO FREEWAY

Santa Monica Mountain

WEST
HOLLYWOOD

Mann's
Chinese
Theater

Hollywood Bowl

Hollywood

Southwest
Museum

Heritage
Square

BEVERLY HILLS

Hollywood Wax Museum

UCLA

Paramount Studios

Studio Museum

Hollywood Memorial Park

Dodger Stadium

Chinatown

Will Rogers State
Historic Park

LA County
Museum of Art

Century
City

Farmers Market

La Brea Tar Pits &
George C Page Museum

LOS ANGELES

HOLLYWOOD FREEWAY

Music
Center

El Pueblo
de Los Angeles
State Historic Park

Little Tokyo

710

SANTA
MONICA

SANTA MONICA FREEWAY

City Hall

Malibu

405

CULVER
CITY

Wells Fargo
History Museum

10

Museum of
Contemporary Art

VENICE

Marina
del
Rey

Exposition Park
(California Museum
of Science & Industry
Los Angeles County
Natural History
Museum)

110

Memorial
Coliseum
& Sports
Arena

MAYWOOD

PLAYA DEL REY

INGLEWOOD

HARBOR FREEWAY

HUNTINGTON
PARK

Los Angeles
International Airport

105

WESTMONT

SOUTH GATE

LYNWOOD

Santa Monica
Bay

1

HAWTHORNE

WILLOWBROOK

LONG BEACH FREEWAY

GARDENA

COMPTON

MANHATTAN BEACH

91

HERMOSA BEACH

SAN

405

CARSON

Los Angeles River

REDONDO BEACH

DIEGO

FREEWAY

710

TORRANCE

South Coast
Botanic Garden

WILMINGTON

LONG
BEACH

Palos Verdes
Peninsula

110

RANCHO
PALOS VERDES

Wayfarers'
Chapel

Marineland

SAN
PEDRO

LOS ANGELES

0   5   10 km

San Pedro
Bay

Accommodation

There is an exhaustive supply of hotels, motels and resorts throughout the Greater Los Angeles area so, as mentioned earlier, you are advised to check location first. Two of the newest hotels are the **Hotel Inter-Continental at California Plaza** with 469 rooms and the **Shutters on the Beach** in Santa Monica with 198 rooms, which opened in 1992 and 1993 respectively. The following is a selection of top of the range recommendations:

Hotel Bel-Air, 701 Stone Canyon Rd (tel: (310) 472 1211). About as exclusive as one can find, this exceptional hostelry only has 92 rooms and suites, all regally appointed. The interior design was re-done in 1982, utilising

Choose from nearly 1500 rooms at the space-age Westin Bonaventure

natural stone and wood-burning fireplaces, and fresh flowers everywhere. The 11 acres (4.5 hectares) of gardens were also improved. The emphasis is on seclusion.

Beverly Hills, 9641 Sunset Blvd (tel: (310) 276 2251). The well-heeled have been in love with this 'pink' palace' since it opened in 1912. It is to re-open in 1995 after extensive renovation. Thanks to 12 acres (5 hectares) of tropical gardens, the hotel and its de-luxe bungalows are well away from the main road. The Coterie restaurant here is plush and pricey, but a salad and a glass of wine in the famous Polo Lounge is affordable.

The Biltmore, 506 S Grand Ave (tel: (310) 624 1011). A de-luxe 683-room landmark that has been modernised and restored to its original grandeur. All the rooms feature traditional French furniture and among the 62 suites is one with its own lift and one with a grand piano. Its restaurant, Bernard's, provides some of the finest dining in Los Angeles, and the Spanish-styled library overlooking Pershing Square has become Rendezvous Court where afternoon tea and drinks are served. Other amenities include a health club with pool.

Four Seasons, 300 S Doheny Drive (tel: (310) 273 2222). This recently opened 179-room stylish Beverly Hills property is a sister hotel to London's Inn on the Park and New York's The Pierre. The rooms, plus 106 suites, are all decorated with antiques; the public rooms with marble and fresh flowers. It's sophisticated and expensive, especially Garden's Restaurant whose dinner menus are particularly eclectic and imaginative. The hotel offers its own terrace pool and café, sauna and jacuzzi, and complimentary limo transport to famous Rodeo Drive.

Lowell, 9291 Burton Way (tel: (310) 278 3344). Re-opens in late 1995. Formerly named L'Ermitage in honour of Russia's Imperial Winter Palace in St Petersburg, this luxurious all-suite hotel may not be everyone's cup of tea even if they can afford its rates. It is open only for guests' use, and that includes its elegant restaurants, Le Brassiere and Diaghlev Lounge. Many of the suites (143 in total) are split-level and all are beautifully furnished. Service is first class and amenities include a rooftop garden, pool and spa, and free chauffeured Rolls for excursions within Beverly Hills.

Radisson Hollywood Roosevelt, 7000 Hollywood Blvd (tel: (213) 466 7000). There is a lot of movie history attached to this 328-room, suite and cabana Hollywood hotel. It's been a landmark since 1927 when it hosted the first Academy Awards, and for many years was *the* place to be seen. Errol Flynn, Ernest Hemingway and Shirley Temple are just three of the host of celebrities who have been guests here. Recent renovation has put a fresh gleam on the Spanish colonial lobby with its painted ceiling and the famous Cinegrill restaurant. Facilities include an Olympic-sized pool in the garden.

Regent Beverly Wilshire, 9500 Wilshire Blvd (tel: (310) 275 5200). A grand dame of a hotel whose Beaux Arts façade was designed in 1928 with a later wing added in 1971. Now a Regent hotel (the company has given it many improvements), it is as handsome and as luxurious as ever.

The Westin Bonaventure, 404 S Figueroa St (tel: (213) 624 1000). John Portman designed this hotel comprising five gold-glassed cylindrical towers back in the 1970s. Its architecture continues to be admired and it is well used by business travellers and conventioners. If you like the large and spectacular this is an excellent (but pricey) downtown base. There are 1,368 guest rooms and eight levels of shops and restaurants. Guests receive special rates for the YMCA fitness center.

Restaurants

Downtown, there are fun Mexican restaurants around Olvera Street, Chinese delights in Chinatown, and Japanese delicacies in Little Tokyo. Among the recommendations in the area are:

Clifton's Silver Spoon Cafeteria, 515 W 7th St (tel: (213) 485 1814). A good bet for brunch, this elegant but inexpensive cafeteria has a turn-of-the-century setting. Imaginative soups and salads come from the basement Soup Kitchen; other inventive American fare from the Meditation Room.

Cole's P.E. Buffet, 118 E 6th St (tel: (213) 622 4090). For years a favourite for a sandwich lunch, and still cheap. It is said the French Dip sandwich was invented here, and other choices include roast beef, corned beef and pastrami.

Mon Kee's, 679 N Spring St (tel: (213) 628 6717). A cheerfully crowded and chaotic Chinese restaurant that is notable for its fresh seafood – alive before you order it. Specialities include crab and shrimp in spicy salt.

The Tower 1150 S Olive St (tel: (213) 746 1554). A room with a view atop the Transamerica Center. This restaurant is expensive, but worth it with classical French cuisine.

Around the mid Wilshire Boulevard area are:

Canter's Fairfax Restaurant, Delicatessen and Bakery, 419 N Fairfax Ave (tel: (213) 651 2030). Probably the largest and liveliest deli on this avenue, it's very Jewish and open 24 hours. It hasn't changed for years, and is still easy on the pocket.

El Cholo, 1121 S Western Ave (tel: (213) 734 2773). Clark Gable used to eat at this classical Mexican place (one of a chain). It has been serving enormous *margaritas* and *tortillas* for 60 years and does have that hacienda atmosphere it emulates.

Pacific Dining Car, 1310 W 6th St (tel: (213) 483 6000). Prime beef and an excellent wine list give this former railway car its deserved reputation as a restaurant. It is open 24 hours.

There are plenty of interesting restaurants and fast food outlets along Melrose Avenue. But also in Hollywood are:

Citrus, 6703 Melrose Ave (tel: (213) 857 0034). Chef Michel Richard creates French-Californian cuisine that continues to delight enthusiastic foodies. The restaurant is pleasant and airy and the prices are high.

Columbia Bar & Grill, 1448 N Gower St (tel: (213) 461 8800). CBS and other studio types are often to be found lunching here on typically American fare like crab cakes and chilli. Prices are moderate and the airy restaurant has a patio section.

Eating is one of the main charms in Beverly Hills. Recommendations include:
The Bistro, 246 N Canon Drive (tel: (310) 273 5633). One of the socialities' gathering places – a place to see and be seen surrounded by *Irma la Douce* décor. Very pricey, but there is superb continental cuisine.
Café Rodeo (Beverly Rodeo Hotel), 360 N Rodeo Drive (tel: (213) 273 0300). People-watch from the open front here. A moderate price pays for a great salad.
Matsuhisa, 129 N La Cienega Blvd (tel: (310) 659 9639). Thought by many to be the best Japanese restaurant outside of Japan, but be prepared to pay for it.
La Scala, 9455 Santa Monica Blvd (tel: (213) 275 0579). Still considered one of LA's best restaurants, La Scala attracts the famous with a penchant for Italian fare. Expensive but exquisite pasta and pastries and chicken *cacciatore* are amongst the offerings.

In Santa Monica are:
Border Grill, 1445 4th St (tel: (310) 451 1655). This is the closest you can come to gourmet Mexican dining. The food is always innovative and exciting even if the noise levels are at times painful.
Chinois on Main, 2709 Main St (tel: (310) 392 9025). Wolfgang Puck's sensational Pacific Rim cuisine consistently gets rave reviews. The noise levels can be as stratospheric as the prices.

Shopping
In two words, no shortage. Among the most appealing complexes around town are:
Beverly Center, Beverly Blvd. LA's largest; three levels of stores, restaurants and cinemas atop four levels of parking lots make up the Beverly Center. This is the location of the Hard Rock Café, the Irvine Ranch Farmers' Market and a number of boutiques that include Rodier.
Century City Shopping Center and Marketplace, 10250 Santa Monica Blvd. An early Los Angeles mall that has been smartened up. It now covers 18 acres (7 hectares) and features 140 shops including branches of Bullocks and Broadway. The major attraction is Gelson's market.
El Mercado, 3425 E 1st St. There is a real Mexican flavour at this complex, which is a mixture of a food market, shops and restaurants. Mariachis (strolling Mexican musicians) add to the atmosphere as they play on the mezzanine. Stalls on the main floor sell ingredients to whip up a Mexican meal, and are surrounded by a tortillaria, bakery, snack bars and delis. Crafts can be found in the basement.
Fashion Square Sherman Oaks, between Woodman and Hazeltine on Riverside Drive, Sherman Oaks – one of the area's early large shopping

plazas. Brick-paved outdoor promenades are lined with quality shops, anchored at each end by Bullocks and The Broadway department stores.

Fisherman's Village, Fiji Way, Marina del Rey – a collection of quaint restaurants and shops next to the marina and cruise departure point for harbour excursions.

Fisherman's Wharf, Redondo Beach – a cluster of unusual shops that line the path to the end of the pier. There are also souvenir stands and stalls selling fresh fish.

Garment District in downtown LA offers all kinds of discount stores for fashions, along Los Angeles Street from 7th Street to Washington Boulevard. Many fashion bargains are on offer in the retail outlets located within the Cooper Building here, and good prices on quality men's suits can be found across the street in Academy Award Clothes.

Japanese Village Plaza, bounded by 1st and 2nd Sts, San Pedro and Central Ave. This cleverly designed complex has white stucco, inset stone paths and ponds, and a traditional fireman's lookout tower as its landmark. A variety of stores and restaurants are to be found here, many concentrating on Japanese food and goods.

La Brea Avenue, around the junction with Melrose Ave and Wilshire Blvd. Many art galleries are moving into this part of town, adding a smart dimension to what was an odd mixture of car dealers and commercial buildings. Leading galleries include Wenger, Whiteley and Jan Baum.

L A City Mall, N Los Angeles St. This well-landscaped, multi-level mall was built in the 1970s. It has plenty of room to park, a plaza with shops and restaurants and a pedestrian bridge above Temple Street.

Melrose Avenue, Hollywood. A lively avenue where you can find anything from used clothing to new and radical fashions, trendy design stores and galleries. Parking is difficult especially at weekends when shoppers come in droves. Wear good walking shoes for the 3-mile (5km) stroll from Highland East to Dohony.

Olvera Street, between Sunset Blvd, Main St, the Plaza and Los Angeles St. This is the heart of downtown LA, with Mexican overtones. Shops and stalls specialise in Mexican crafts and

Shops in LA can be as eye-catching as their contents

food – made on the spot or imported.

Ports O'Call Village, San Pedro. A complex at the harbour's edge that combines a re-created New England fishing village and a Mediterranean one – both featuring shops and restaurants. Harbour cruises available.

Rodeo Drive, Beverly Hills. Come, if only to window shop at this celebrated purchaser's paradise. Boutiques stock designer labels like Hermes, Ted Lapidus, Ungaro and Louis Vuitton.

Shoreline Village, Long Beach. A cute re-creation of a historical waterfront village with bijou stores and restaurants.

Town and Country Shopping Center, 17200 Ventura Blvd, Encino. Two plazas and complexes on different levels are enhanced by first-class landscaping. A villagey feel to this centre may be helped by the unusual absence of large department stores.

Westside Pavilion at Pico and Westwood Blvds. An indoor modern mall with an airy atrium, though its design also borrows from the arcaded structures of the last century. Between the Nordstrom and Robinsons-May department stores are three levels of boutiques offering a mix of clothes, gifts and fast food.

Children
A Universal Studios Hollywood tour has to be the prime attraction for children staying in Los Angeles. Griffith Park containing Gene Autrey's

Western Heritage Museum, Griffith Observatory, Los Angeles Zoo and the Travel Town collection of railway engines is a firm favourite too. Downtown, on Main Street, the Los Angeles Children's Museum (the hands-on variety) is specifically designed for youngsters, as is the Long Beach Children's Museum on Long Beach Boulevard.

Los Angeles has many museums which will appeal to younger members of the family, often related to the screen stars. The Hollywood Wax Museum, for example, on Hollywood Boulevard, is full of replicas, and you can see how the stars were coiffed and made-up at the Max Factor Museum of Beauty on North Highland Avenue. On that same avenue, the Hollywood Studio Museum displays photographs and other exhibits

Children are sure to appreciate the old carousel on Santa Monica pier – straight out of the film *The Sting* – and may have to be dragged from the Children's Book and Music Center on Santa Monica Boulevard (on some Saturdays there are story hours). Day excursions to Six Flags Magic Mountain theme park and to Disneyland are both possible.

All the fun of the film set. A Universal Studios Hollywood tour makes an unforgettable day out

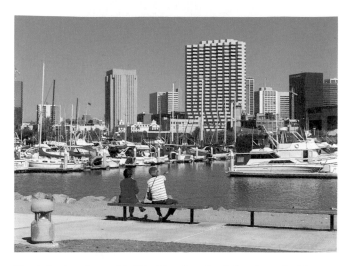

The skyline has changed, but San Diego has attracted seafarers for 400 years

SAN DIEGO

There are many reasons for wanting to come to California's birthplace. It is the state's southernmost town, so close to Mexico that popping across the border is considered an afternoon's excursion. It has a near-perfect climate and a premier location between mountains and sea, not to mention a wonderful natural harbour, which completes its appeal to watersport enthusiasts. San Diego's colours are clear, and its lifestyle relaxed, despite its city size. With its heritage, one of America's finest marine parks and a world-famous zoo, plus excellent food and lodging, San Diego can claim to be a true family vacation centre.

A Portuguese explorer, Juan Rodriguez Cabrillo, was the first to sail into the Bay in the 1540s, though it was Sebastian Vizcaino who bestowed the city's name some 60 years later. It was here that Father Junipero Serra founded the very first of the chain of Missions in 1769, and Mexico made it the capital in 1825. Once the Americans had raised their flag, however, San Diego developed less quickly than Los Angeles and San Francisco, and remained villagey until the railroad arrived and the US Navy (who are still here) made it a base. After the last World War, the aerospace industries moved to the area – one of the earliest sophisticated rockets was created here.

In the past few years, sleek mirrored skyscrapers have sprung up downtown alongside the dramatic Horton

SAN DIEGO

Plaza shopping centre. The 1980s saw a substantial number of new hotels and restaurants, and the reopening of the Old Globe Theatre which offers year-round professional theatre. The decade turned with the opening of a new convention centre and increased accommodation. By car Los Angeles is only 125 miles (201km) away. The international airport is near downtown and is served by 20 plus airlines. A rail service from LA pulls into the Santa Fe depot downtown. Several bus routes criss-cross the city and operate to the Mexican border, so does the San Diego Trolley. Taxis and rental cars are readily available.

A Sporting City

Since it is a city built around water, with 70 miles (112km) of beaches, San Diego is famous for watersports, particularly year-round ocean fishing. Fitness programmes are also a part of daily life in San Diego, and there are over 70 golf courses and 1,200 tennis courts in the county. The Jack Murphy Stadium is home for the San Diego Padres baseball team, the Chargers football team and Clippers basketball team. In winter, whale watching has become an increasingly popular attraction – between mid-December and mid-February some 12,000 grey whales pass the coast here, heading for the warm breeding grounds of Baja California. The viewing is free at the station at Cabrillo National Monument (after admission to the monument) and expeditions can be made for a closer look by boat. Because Mexico is so close, most visitors here make the trip across the border. You may need a tourist card – if only to shop (US dollars are usually accepted). There are two crossing points: at San Ysidro and at Otay Mesa.

Windsurfing in the Bay

WHAT TO SEE IN AND AROUND SAN DIEGO

◆◆◆
BALBOA PARK ✓

This park, the pride of San Diego, has the 1915–16 Panama-California Exposition to thank for its present structure. Although the land had been set aside by the city in 1868 and an ex-school-teacher was planting trees in 1889, the Moorish and Spanish-style buildings were erected especially for the exhibition and added to for the subsequent 1935–36 California Pacific International Exposition. Today, the 1,149 acres (465 hectares) encompasses theatres, museums, art galleries and the zoo. The most prominent landmark is **California Tower** whose 100-bell carillon chimes every 15 minutes. Anyone who has been to Mexico City will be reminded of the famous cathedral there when they look at **The California Building**, though the latter is decorated with statues of those relevant to San Diego's own history, like Cabrillo. Across the way, the small garden is modelled after Spain's Alcazar.

Another replica is that of Shakespeare's **Globe Theatre**; this one was constructed in 1935. The local outcry was so great at the thought of the playhouse being demolished when the Exposition ended, it was made into a permanent structure, a complex which today features contemporary dramas alongside the Bard's, in three theatres.

Balboa Park: the California Tower from the Alcazar Garden

Balboa Park also has San Diego's major museums. The handsome tiled Spanish Renaissance villa for example, houses the **San Diego Museum of Art**. Its highlights are the superb examples of Spanish and Italian art, but its collection also includes other Old Masters, modern American contributions and an Oriental gallery. Closed Mondays. In the adjacent **Timken Art Gallery**, art lovers will find an assortment of paintings and interesting Russian icons. Remains of this area's earliest inhabitants are housed in the **Museum of Man** in the California Tower, including those of the 3,000-year-old Kumeyaay Indians and the 5,000-year-old Del Mar Man. Exhibits showing the southwest's desert and marine life are displayed in the **Natural History Museum**. In contrast, the **Aerospace Museum** concentrates on San Diego's involvement with aviation development. Another favourite venue is the **Reuben H Fleet Space Theater and Science Center** (see under **Children**). Smaller specialist museums are also located in Balboa: the **Museum of San Diego History**; the **Museum of Photographic Arts**, featuring changing exhibits by noted photographers; the **Hall of Champions**, which pays tribute to local sportsmen and athletes; and the **Model Railroad Museum,** featuring miniature trains.

Balboa is not only about culture, however. There are craft shops near the **Zoo**, a famous attraction with almost 4,000 animals (see under **Children**), and an organ pavilion with outdoor Sunday concerts. On weekends, street entertainers are drawn to the central plaza and there are horse-drawn carriages.

◆

CORONADO AND EMBARCADERO

The Hotel del Coronado, in Coronado, insists that it is more than mere rumour that the Duke of Windsor first met Wallis Simpson there. It certainly has hosted many celebrities in its time – that's since the 1880s. Coronado is virtually an island in the Bay, but it is attached by a narrow strip of land called the Silver Strand, stretching from Imperial Beach to the Coronado peninsula.

On the main waterfront, at the foot of Harbor Drive, **Seaport Village's** shops and restaurants are a pleasant way of passing time, or you might watch the activity from the Harbor Seafood Mart whilst eating.

Also along the Embarcadero is the **Maritime Museum**, housing the 1898 steam-powered ferry *Berkeley* and the 1863 sailing ship, *Star of India*.

◆◆

GASLAMP QUARTER
5th Ave
A 16-block, 38-acre (15-hectare) National Historic

A killer whale – the big attraction at Sea World in Mission Bay Park

and recreation area where you can charter a fishing boat, swim, waterski, sunbathe, cycle and picnic. For families, the prime reason for coming to the park is to see **Sea World**, a 150-acre (61-hectare) wonderland of marine life. There are aquariums, exhibits, shows and America's largest collection of waterfowl. Among places to head for are the petting pool (where the animals may be touched), the live shark pool, the sea otter habitat, the walrus pool and the dolphin pool. But tops is the Shamu stadium, recently enlarged, home to the park's killer whales – the real star attraction. The complex also incorporates an educational facility called 'Places of Learning'. One not-to-be-missed exhibit, between the shows, is 'Penguin Encounter', with over 400 Antarctic penguins representing seven species. The newest exhibit is 'Forbidden Reef' featuring 'Bat Ray Shallows' and 'Moray Eel Caverns'.

District, recommended for arts and crafts browsers, stretching from Broadway to the waterfront. When entrepreneurial Alonz Horton purchased the property in 1857 it was with the idea of relocating the city centre closer to the ocean. 'New Town', as it was called then, did flourish in the late 19th century but later fell into decline. Its Victorian-era buildings are now mostly art galleries, antique shops and restaurants. Walking tours Saturdays from Island Avenue.

◆◆◆
MISSION BAY PARK
Once a marshland, today, this is an enormous aquatic park

◆◆◆
MISSION SAN DIEGO DE ALCALA
10818 San Diego Mission Rd
This, the first of the Mission chain, was founded in 1769 on Presidio Hill. It was moved to its present location, 6 miles (10km) up the valley, in 1774, to take advantage of a good water supply. Inside the Mission, today, is the **Father**

A Spanish-style façade – one of many reminders that San Diego is on Mexico's doorstep

Luis Jayme Museum, which contains a number of relics of early Mission days, including Father Serra's own handwritten records. Presidio Hill itself rises above the entrance to Mission Valley and is now a 40-acre (16-hectare) landscaped park, and location of the **Junipero Serra Museum** (closed Mondays) with superb views over the Pacific Ocean, Mission Bay and Mission Valley.

OLD TOWN

Mason St and San Diego Ave
Until 1821 Presidio Hill was the San Diego centre, but when it became too crowded settlers moved to the base of the hill. Today, this 12-acre (5-hectare) district is a restored State Historic Park to be toured by foot on your own or as part of an organised tour. The setting and atmosphere is of the Mexican and early American periods with buildings dating from 1829 to 1869. Among those to see are **Casa de Las Estudillo** (1830), constructed from logs brought down from the mountains and rawhide to secure the beams, and the **Machado y Stewart** adobe house. **Casa de Altamirano**, a New-England-style frame house, contains a newspaper museum, whilst Seeley Stable has Western memorabilia and horse-drawn vehicles. The **Whaley House** (1857) was the city's first luxury brick home and has been refurnished with antiques and furniture of the period. It was here that the American flag was first raised in 1846.

Some of the buildings have been turned into gift boutiques and early-California-style restaurants. You'll find several around Squibob Square and at Bazaar del Mundo, as well as in **Heritage Park**, where the influence is Victorian.

POINT LOMA

This is the location of the **Cabrillo National Monument** honouring that explorer's 1542

discovery. You can learn
everything you need to know
at the Visitors' Center and
enjoy a marvellous view of San
Diego Bay. The best place for
whale spotting is the
observatory behind the
lighthouse. Between mid-
December and mid-February
each year, thousands of
California greys head south
from here. The point is 10
miles (16km) west of the city,
reached on Catalina
Boulevard. Monument open
daily.

Accommodation
A wide range of
accommodation is available,
but you should choose by
area. Downtown/Balboa Park is

one area, for example; Mission
Valley (colloquially called
Hotel Circle), another. Then
there are Harbor Island and
Shelter Island, both close to the
airport. Among the places
recommended are:
Hotel del Coronado, 1500
Orange Ave, Coronado (tel:
(619) 522 8000) – a hotel with a
certain cachet, located on
Coronado Island, linked by
causeway to the mainland. It
has hosted princes (hence the
Prince of Wales Grill), but
there are alternative places to
eat including an American deli.
There are 680 rooms, a pool
and tennis on the property.
Humphrey's Half Moon Inn,
2303 Shelter Island Drive (tel:
(619) 224 3411) – a smallish

hotel with 182 rooms and a restaurant that features seafood and overlooks the bay.

Hyatt Islandia on Mission Bay, 1441 Quivira Rd (tel: (619) 224 1234) – a 423-room hotel on Mission Bay with comfortable lanai (rooms with patios) and tower rooms. Its coffee garden eating-place has a pleasant setting and the hotel's own marina rents out sailing boats.

The Westgate, 1055 2nd Ave (tel: (619) 238 1818) – a luxurious 223-room hotel in the heart of town across from the Horton Plaza shopping centre, where many rooms offer Bay and harbour views. Its Le Fontainebleau French restaurant has won many awards and there is nightly entertainment in the Plaza Lounge.

Selected bed and breakfast accommodation includes:

Balboa Park Inn, 3402 Park Blvd (tel: (619) 298 0823) – conveniently located within walking distance of the Zoo. Some of the 25 rooms have fireplaces and in-room jacuzzis. Local telephone calls are free and Continental breakfast is included in the price.

Coronado Village Inn, 1017 Park Place, Coronado (tel: (619) 435 9318) – 20 rooms in a European-style resort hotel where you can get budget bed and breakfast. It is within easy reach of the Hotel del Coronado and the beach.

Heritage Park Inn, 2470 Heritage Park Row (tel: (619) 299 6832) – a restored Queen Anne mansion in the centre of town, with 9 rooms. Full breakfasts are served and film classics shown nightly, also evening refreshments and candlelight dinners available.

Restaurants

Recommendations include:

Anthony's Star of the Sea Room, 1360 Harbor Island Drive at Ash (tel: (619) 232 7408) – open only for cocktails and dinner, this expensive seafood restaurant is probably still *the* restaurant in San Diego when it comes to fish. It also offers a superb view of the Bay and Point Loma.

Belgian Lion, 2265 Bacon St, off W Point Loma Blvd (tel: (619) 223 2700). A charming European-style restaurant serving creative French cuisine; dinner only. During the week the *prix fixe* dinners are the best value in town.

Casa de Pico, 2754 Calhoun St (tel: (619) 296 3267) – almost a must for lunch, if not for dinner, this Mexican restaurant is in Bazaar del Mundo in the heart of Old Town. The dishes are traditional and reasonably priced and you may choose to eat inside or in the flower-bedecked courtyard.

Shopping

San Diego has both major centres and themed complexes. Among them are:

Bazaar del Mundo, 2754 Calhoun St – in the heart of Old Town, this is a favourite and colourful *mélange* of shops and restaurants,

somewhat Mexican influenced.
Belmont Park, Ventura and
Mission Blvd – shopping,
dining and entertainment.
Farmers Bazaar, 245 Seventh
Ave – speciality shops and
fresh produce.
Fashion Valley, 352 Fashion
Valley Rd - a landscaped
centre whose 148 shops and
six major department stores
specialise in high-fashion.
Gaslamp Quarter, between
Broadway and Harbor and 4th,
5th and 6th Aves – a 16-block
downtown renovated Victorian
district where you'll find

*If you want to get ahead... visit one
of the city's many department stores*

interesting boutiques, art
galleries and restaurants.
Horton Plaza – a modern,
innovative, multi-level complex
in downtown San Diego with
department stores, speciality
shops, restaurants, a cinema,
theatres, a farmers' market.
Daily entertainment a feature.
Mission Valley Center, 1640
Camino del Rio North – the
largest most accessible
shopping centre where you'll
find classy department
stores, like Bullock's and
Robinsons-May, as well as 150
speciality shops and
restaurants.
Old Town Esplanade, 2461
San Diego Ave – Old Town's

SAN DIEGO

The 'wild man' of the jungle – an orang-utan at San Diego Zoo

new centre of interest which simulates a Mexican market-place and sells giftware from around the world.

Paladion San Diego, 777 Front St – a collection of the world's finest stores including Tiffany, Cartier, Gucci and Gianni Versace.

Promenade at Pacific Beach, 4150 Mission Blvd – shops, galleries and eating places in a Mediterranean setting.

Seaport Village, 849 W Harbor Drive – a re-created version of an old Californian seaside town on San Diego Bay, with 75 'individual' shops and restaurants plus a restored 1890 carousel.

Squibob Square, 2611 San Diego Ave – a collection of speciality shops with Western-style fronts in Old Town State Historic Park.

Children

The **San Diego Zoo** is tops with any child, in particular the area with miniature animals. Located in Balboa Park, the zoo is world-renowned and noted for its many rare and exotic species; aerial tram ride included in admission. **Sea World** in Mission Bay Park equally delights with killer whales starring in their new stadium (see also **What to See**). The **Reuben H Fleet Space Theater and Science Center**, in Balboa Park, is another recommendation. Here, a giant OMNIMAX projector, planetarium equipment and specially built screen surrounds the visitor with colour, light and sound. The same building houses a fascinating 'please touch' science centre.

PALM SPRINGS AND THE DESERT COMMUNITIES

Palm Springs is what it has always been – an oasis in the desert. Thanks to an invasion of film stars escaping the hassles of Hollywood in the 1920s and 30s, it has become a very rich oasis, with high property values, glossy shops and many golf courses. In recent years, it has sprouted satellite 'oases' (such as Indian Wells, La Quinta and Rancho Mirage) on its fringes. These are collectively known as the Desert Communities.

It was the Indians who discovered the hot springs in the first place, long before the Spanish arrived in 1774, so perhaps it is appropriate that much of the land today is owned by their descendants. Those who live here, though, aren't short of cash either: past and present inhabitants include Bob Hope, Gerald Ford, Chaplin's son and Sonny Buono. Walter Annenberg's estate (where the Duke and Duchess of York stayed during their 1988 visit) is so vast it has its own golf course.

The weather is the Desert's biggest attraction, especially the winter temperatures, usually in the 70s or 80s F (20s or low 30s C). The Santa Rosa and San Jacinto mountains protect Palm Springs from the sea coast's clouds and fog and there's no industry to pollute the air. Vegetation is used cleverly for landscaping – mesquite trees, a profusion of oleanders, a carpet of purple verbena – but local residents do give their olive trees a 'poodle cut' to prevent a mess when the trees scatter their fruit. Local residents are also particular about signs – anything that is garish, such as

An oasis for the well-heeled, Palm Springs lives up to its name

neon, is forbidden, so Palm Springs' McDonald's appears very sedate without its drive-up windows and its giant yellow arches. (Such sign laws, however, do not apply to the surrounding communities.) Palm Springs and the Desert Communities are practically synonymous with golf – everywhere you look there's a course. Among the more unusual are La Quinta Citrus Course (so called because it is surrounded by citrus trees), and the course nicknamed 'golf on the rocks' because it looks like Alcatraz in the desert, surrounded by water, against a mountain backdrop. It costs $200,000 (each year) to grass seed each course and it takes a million gallons (4.5 million litres) of water a day to keep it green.

Water, of course, comes from the mountains when the snow melts, and there are 26 wells in the area. Indian Wells, for example, was so named because the Indians had wells close to the ground's surface.

Golf Crazy!

Visiting and resident celebrities play golf; others come to watch the tournaments whose winners pick up hefty prizes. Palm Springs is so golf crazy it even holds an annual golf-cart parade! But there is other sport, too – tennis, riding, and hiking – plus the newest fashion, ballooning. Several companies offer one hour flights, usually just after sunrise or just before sunset when desert weather conditions are at their best. In the film *Lost Horizons*, Palm Springs was used as the locality of 'Shangri La' – tranquil, beautiful, majestic, inaccessible, although these days the desert oasis is easy to reach by road or air from Los Angeles.

WHAT TO SEE IN AND AROUND PALM SPRINGS

AERIAL TRAMWAY

This is Palm Springs' major attraction, operating year-round from the 2,643ft (805m)-high Valley Station to the mountain lodge level of Mount San Jacinto State Park and Wilderness, at 8,516ft (2,595m). In summer, hikers use it, in winter the skiers come. 'Crocker's Dream', a 22-minute film depicting the tram's history, is screened throughout the day for free in the lower level theatre of the Mountain Station. There is a ride charge though to reach the top where there is a buffet-style restaurant and a bar and picnic area. It was electrical engineer, Francis Crocker, in the 1930s, who insisted that a tramway could be constructed in rugged Chino Canyon to allow people to retreat from the excessive summer heat, but his dream wasn't fulfilled until 1963.

Outdoor enthusiasts today can use (in summer) as many and as much as they like of the 54 miles (87km) of hiking trails in Mount San Jacinto State Park and Wilderness. The really keen might opt for the 5½-mile (9km) trek to the peak; the less intrepid can hire a mule or

The Joshua Tree National Park – a vast area northeast of Palm Springs

stick to the one-mile-long (1.6km) nature walk through pleasant Long Valley, where a permanent ranger station is located. Throughout the Wilderness area, there are five designated camping grounds (permit required); there are also short guided trails and longer guided walks.

In winter, the area is perfect for cross-country skiers who can rent equipment and take instruction at the Nordi Ski Center, open from mid-November to mid-April. The more adventurous can rent snowshoes for treks into the Wilderness and even snow camp. Valley Station is on Tramway Road, 3½ miles (6km) southwest of Highway 111.

◆◆
INDIAN CANYONS
S Palm Canyon Drive
For a nominal fee, this Indian-owned land (closed early July to early September) may be explored by car, on horseback or as part of an organised expedition on foot. There are many beauty spots, often used as film backdrops. One of the best known is Palm Canyon. It extends for 15 miles (24km) through a series of rock gorges and minor canyons, but may be reached by an easy footpath. For equestrians, the scenic trail to Andreas Canyon is recommended. The nearest of the canyons to Palm Springs is Tahquitz – a foot trail which starts within city limits and leads to Tahquitz Falls.

♦♦♦
LIVING DESERT

47–900 Portola Ave, Palm Desert
This enormous slice of desert may
be reached in a 25-minute drive
east from the city and is both a
wildlife park and botanical garden.
Animals in the habitat include
bighorn sheep and coyotes, and
there are also hundreds of exotic
desert plants on display (some
for sale). Self-guided nature trails
as well as picnic sites are added
features of this popular
excursion. Closed mid-June to
August.

♦♦
MOORTEN'S BOTANICAL GARDEN

1701 S Palm Canyon Drive
More than 3,000 varieties of
desert plant growing here prove
that the desert is not that harsh.
For a small fee, visitors can take
self-guided trails past some
exciting desert sights.

♦♦
PALM SPRINGS DESERT MUSEUM

101 Museum Drive
Against the backdrop of Mount
San Jacinto, this 20-acre (8-
hectare) facility features dioramas
and displays that relate to the
locality, as well as changing
exhibitions and science
programmes. On the same site,
the Annenberg Theater features a
host of top-name performers.
Closed Mondays and May to mid-
September. Free on the first
Friday of each month.

The Desert Communities

◆
CATHEDRAL CITY
From a mere 'bedroom' community for neighbouring Palm Springs, Cathedral City has achieved its own identity, though it is still being developed. Its accommodation is more reasonably priced. The Desert Dixieland Jazz Festival is held here each April/May.

◆
DESERT HOT SPRINGS
A 10-minute drive from Aerial Tramway, this community has its own lodgings, restaurants and shops, and sport facilities that include three public golf courses. It also has its own museum – **Cabot's Old Indian Pueblo Museum** – which houses a collection of early-day relics, including a shield from the Custer battlefield. Closed Mondays and Tuesdays.

◆
INDIO
One of the oldest communities in the Coachella Valley, Indio is set amid date palms. The first National Date Festival was held here in 1921 and is repeated each February. Another claim to fame is reflected in its title 'Winter Polo Capital of the West'. Week-long activities include ostrich and camel races, and an Arabian Nights pageant.

◆
PALM DESERT
A plush valley community, Palm Desert is home to the hotel chain Marriott's amazing resort and spa (for which sand was imported from Israel and for which the girls steering the lagoon boats received instruction from the US coastguards!). The McCallum Theater for the Performing Arts, part of the Bob Hope Cultural Center, and the multi-million dollar town-centre mall and exclusive El Paseo shops are other attractions here.

◆
LA QUINTA
La Quinta probably has more golf holes per square mile than any other city. Here is the Western home of American golf – PCA West – whose championship courses have been designed by Pete Dye, Jack Nicklaus and Arnold Palmer, and are used for prestigious tournaments such as The Skins Game and the PGA Club Professional Championship. Famous La Quinta Hotel was an exclusive retreat in the 1930s and has hosted many screen celebrities. When the community was incorporated as a city in 1982, ceremonies were held on this hotel's lawn.

◆
RANCHO MIRAGE
A prestigious place to live and stay. There are ritzy hotels like the Ritz-Carlton and Westin Mission Hills Resort, and ritzy houses like that belonging to Frank Sinatra (which has a model railway in its grounds).

Accommodation
Most of the desert hotels are true American resorts and there has been an increasing number of very fine ones since Gene Autry financed his first

PALM SPRINGS

hostelry. Among the most lavish are:

Hyatt Grand Champions Resort, 44-600 Indian Wells Lane, Indian Wells (tel: (619) 341 1000). Nearly 300 of the 336 guest rooms are split-level parlour suites, but there are also 20 garden villas which have private butler service and their own spa pool. Recreational facilities include a health and fitness centre, four pools and 12 tennis courts.

Marriott's Desert Springs Resort and Spa, 74-855 Country Club Drive, Palm Desert (tel: (619) 341 2211). This mega resort spreads itself over 400 acres (162 hectares) and has 895 guest rooms. The design incorporates lagoons via which guests are ferried from point to point in small canopied boats, if they don't choose to walk.

Other major resort features include a man-made beach, three swimming pools, two 18-hole golf courses, 16 tennis courts and a fully equipped health spa.

La Quinta Hotel Golf and Tennis Resort, 49-499 Eisenhower Drive, La Quinta (tel: (619) 564 4111). Legendary since 1926, La Quinta's 640 guest rooms are in Spanish-style cottages scattered over 26 acres (10 hectares). This hotel is particularly noted for its buffet lunches and its tennis facilities – 30 hard courts, six grass courts and three clay.

Westin Mission Hills Resort, 71-333 Dinah Shore Drive, Rancho Mirage (tel: (619) 328 5955). More intimate, this hotel's 512 guest rooms are housed in low Moroccan-style buildings with either balcony or terrace views of the golf courses or mountains.

Restaurants

Between Cathedral City and Palm Desert, in Rancho Mirage, is an area known as 'Restaurant Row'. Among the many establishments worth trying are:

Las Casuelas Nuevas, 70-050 Highway 111 (tel: (714) 328 8844). It's large, it's Mexican and it's reasonable. Decorated with hanging plants, a fountain, tall Mexican chairs and oak-topped tables, this is the very place for a 'house plate' – *enchilada*, *tamale*, *taco*, *chilli con carne* and beans or rice. Accompany your meal with popular Mexican beers or *margaritas*.

The Wilde Goose, 67-938 E Palm Canyon Drive (tel: (619) 328 5775). This restaurant has won many awards for its creative cuisine. If you're not ready for roast goose, buffalo meat, venison or the even more exotic wild boar or alligator, there's always roast duck prepared five different ways, prime rib and Beef Wellington. Rustic decor, speciality drinks and entrée prices that start under $20 add to the charm.

Shopping

You can shop till you drop in the desert's many fine stores, boutiques and shops that offer everything from a simple T-shirt to *haute-couture*. Palm Springs' elegant **Palm Canyon Drive** is lined with 1,200 palm trees that are illuminated at

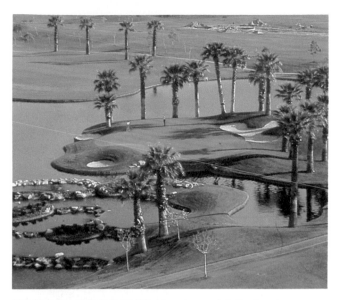

Marriott's Desert Springs provide a luxurious oasis in the desert

night. Its **Desert Fashion Plaza** houses many exclusive stores, speciality shops and fashion boutiques. Pride of place, however, goes to Palm Desert's two-mile (3.2km) long **El Paseo** – the 'Rodeo Drive of the desert'. Among the world's most fashionable shopping streets, its speciality stores include:

Air Dreams, 73-990 El Paseo – this place combines art with fashion. It's an art studio that specialises in limited-edition, hand-painted designs on T-shirts and dresses. All clothes are washable and epitomise the Desert lifestyle.

Diane Freis, 73-255 El Paseo – well-known American designer, Diane Freis' Desert shop features limited-edition dresses in lightweight polyester georgette as well as fashion scarves.

Richard Danskin Galleries, 73-111 El Paseo – here you can buy realistic countryside and horse paintings by Danskin. Also look for desert scenes by local artists.

Children

Recommended for youngsters is the **Palm Springs Oasis Waterpark** on the Gene Autry Trail, Palm Springs, open from mid-March to early September and weekends through to October. There is an admission charge but children under 1ft 3in (1m) can come for free. Major features are the huge wave pool and the freefall and speed slide.

NAPA VALLEY

Just north of San Francisco, Napa Valley is best known for wine. There are countless vineyards which may be visited, and their end products sampled. In addition to the 200 plus wineries, there are 2,500 guest rooms, many restaurants, sport facilities and spas. Mount St Helena, at 4,344ft (1,324m), dominates the landscape and is thought to be an extinct cinder cone, a type of volcano. When it erupted millions of years ago, it uprooted gigantic redwoods and petrified them with its hot ash. Nowadays you can see the result in the Petrified Forest, which leads from Calistoga over the hill to Santa Rosa. One of the most popular ways of overseeing the region is by balloon. If the weather is right, there is no better idea than floating lazily, high over the vines. Alternatively, from the Calistoga Soaring Center, glider flights are available and the Napa Valley Wine Train offers gourmet dining in Pullman cars during a three-hour tour of the valley.

WHAT TO SEE IN THE NAPA VALLEY

Vineyards thrive in the Napa Valley's 'Mediterranean' climate

◆◆◆
CALISTOGA

At the northern end of the Napa Valley, Calistoga is a noted spa area, first discovered by the Wappo Indians. However, it was a Mormon, Sam Brannan, who recognised that the natural qualities of the hot-water geysers and mineral springs would attract visitors. He gave the town its name in 1859 in honour of both the state and New York's Saratoga. Today, a number of places offer therapeutic treatments including mud baths, steam baths and massages. The

Sharpsteen Museum (free), contains scale-model diorama of early Napa Valley spas, wineries, train depots and original Victorian cottages.

Calistoga's main attraction lies 2 miles (3km) to the north. The geyser '**Old Faithful of California**' is fed by an underground river that heats up to well over boiling point every 40 minutes before spouting water in the air as high as 60ft (18m).

◆◆◆
ST HELENA ✓

Robert Louis Stevenson lived in this small town 10 miles (16km) south of Calistoga, and wrote of his experiences in *Silverado Squatters*. Entrance to the

Silverado Museum in Library Lane is free (closed Mondays). The museum contains memorabilia of the writer's life and work, including first editions and photographs. On Main Street, the Napa Valley Museum focuses on the land, people and industry of the Napa Valley.

Three miles (5km) north of town, on Highway 29, a 1846 water-powered grist mill has been preserved in the **Bale Grist Mill State Historic Park** (mill demonstrations by contacting the park in advance, tel: (707) 963 2236). One mile (1.6km) further north on Highway 29, in **Bothe-Napa Valley State Park**, there are 10 miles (16km) of hiking trails up steep hillsides, leading to groves of redwoods.

WINERIES

Napa Valley has become a respected wine region the world over and has so many wineries it would take days to cover them all. The following offer tours and tastings: Beaulieu (St Helena), Beringer (St Helena), Domaine Chandon (Yountville), Folie a Deux (St Helena), Freemark Abbey (St Helena), Hanns Kornell (St Helena), Charles Krug (St Helena), Louis M Martini (St Helena), Joseph Matthews (Napa), Merlion (St Helena), Robert Mondavi (Oakville), Monticello (Napa), St Supéry (Oakville) and Sterling (Calistoga).
Especially recommended visits are:
Beaulieu – the visitor centre incorporates a small theatre where you can watch an audio-visual presentation on the vineyard's history plus a general introduction to wine-making.

Beringer – the family home, the Rhine House, built in 1877, typifies German architecture. (Many of the first wine-makers were of German descent.) Part of the building houses a visitor and wine-tasting centre, and regular tours are given through the limestone caves that were built in the late

Over 100 varieties of grape are grown in this part of California

1800s by Chinese labourers, as the ideal environment in which to age the wine.

Domaine Chandon – the tour here is somewhat unique for Napa since it covers the making of sparkling wine.

St Supéry – this winery has one of the finest educational winery tours in the valley. Particularly interesting is the 'Smellavision' exhibit where visitors can experience the typical component aromas of wine.

Robert Mondavi – very good guided tours here give a complete overview of the

wine-making process.

Sterling – this is located on a hilltop and reached by cable car. There are marvellous views of the valley and visitors may take themselves on a self-guided tour.

◆◆
YOUNTVILLE

Yountville was named after George Calvert Yount, the first white settler in the Napa Valley. He fell in love with the place in 1831 and, with the help of local Indians, constructed a Kentucky blockhouse (a small fortified building) and mill. In 1855, a surveyor was commissioned to lay out the city. By the time Gottlieb Groezinger established his winery and distillery in 1870 (now a shopping and restaurant complex), Yountville was a thriving farming community. Today, it is still a pleasantly rural tourist attraction.

Accommodation

This region of California is rather special in as much as it boasts a large number of interesting inns and bed and breakfast establishments. Among them are:

Oak Knoll Inn, 2200 E Oak Knoll Ave, Napa (tel: (707) 255 2200). A curious French country-style inn set among vineyards. The four rooms each have a private bathroom and a veranda overlooking the Chardonay vines. There is also a swimming pool and outdoor jacuzzi.

The Pink Mansion, 1415

Foothill Blvd, Calistoga (tel: (707) 942 0558.) Dating from Victorian times, the Pink Mansion features a formal living room with fireplace as well as a dining room and games room. Private bathrooms, large breakfasts and afternoon wine and cheese are offered by the proprietors.

Vintage Inn, 6541 Washington St, Yountville (tel: (707) 944 1112). A rustic 80-room establishment that is actually more like a hotel than an inn.

Wine Way Inn, 1019 Foothill Blvd, Calistoga (tel: (707) 942 0680). A friendly house with six named and prettily decorated guest rooms.

NAPA VALLEY WINERIES

Restaurants

Domaine Chandon, California Drive at Highway 29, Yountville (tel: (707) 944 2893) – an elegant, very French restaurant that is part of the winery. Dishes frequently use wine in their preparation and are designed to complement Domain Chandon's wine.

The French Laundry, Washington St at Creek St (tel: (707) 944 2429) – open only for fixed-price dinner. Dining is leisurely in this old stone building and if you care to wander around the garden between courses, feel free.

Mustards, 7399 St Helena Highway (tel: (707) 944 2424). Serves the finest Californian cuisine at both lunch and dinner. The popularity of the restaurant makes reservations advisable.

Shopping

In the small towns of this area, expect to find country craft and antique shops as well as shops selling just about everything. An interesting complex is **Vintage 1870** in Yountville, a converted winery dating from 1870. Among the boutiques here are:

The Chutney Kitchen – for lunch or purchases of home-made Californian chutneys.

The Country Mouse – a cottagey shop featuring dried flowers and collectables.

Fruit of the Vine – look for Napa Valley silk-screen and embroidered sportswear.

Groezinger Wine Company – the place to stock up on Californian wines and sample them in the wine bar.

SONOMA VALLEY/ RUSSIAN RIVER

The tree-clad shoreline of Lake Sonoma

Like neighbouring Napa, the county of Sonoma has a wealth of vineyards – located in the Valley and along the Russian River. Padre Jose Altimira planted the first vines at the Mission of San Francisco Solano and, when this Mission was closed, General Mariano Vallejo planted vines for his own use. For several years, he competed with Agoston Haraszthy, a Hungarian count who created California's oldest winery, Buena Vista, and who chose Sonoma for its climate, perfect for viticulture. Sonoma was also the place

where the first state flag of California was raised, in June 1846. At that time Mexico was governing the territory and had ordered American settlers out. In order to hasten American occupancy, a small band of rebels took Vallejo prisoner and raised their own home-made flag – a piece of unbleached muslin with a red stripe, a painted grizzly bear and a star, and the words 'California Republic' – in the plaza of Sonoma pueblo. A month later, once the American navy had captured the then capital, Monterey, and claimed California for the US, the 'Bear Flag' was replaced with the 'Stars and Stripes'.

WHAT TO SEE IN THE SONOMA VALLEY/ RUSSIAN RIVER

◆◆
GLEN ELLEN

A hamlet just a few miles west of Sonoma, Glen Ellen was the home of author, Jack London, who wrote more than 50 books including *Valley of the Moon*. Others of his books, like *The Sea Wolf* and *The Call of the Wild*, have become American classics, but it was *Valley of the Moon* that brought fame to this region; the name Sonoma ('many moon's) is said to be of Indian origin.

As a memorial to London, the **Jack London State Historic Park** was established in 1959 where the author's famous 'Beauty Ranch' takes up 803 acres (325 hectares). His widow, Charmain, built 'The House of Happy Walls' in 1922, and this houses many mementoes of London's richly varied life. This park is popular with equestrians – a 3 mile (5km) trail leads to the summit of Sonoma Mountain.

◆◆
LACHRYMA MONTIS

This is the name of General Vallejo's 20-acre (8-hectare) estate, which he moved to after he left his adobe home, Casa Grande, on Sonoma's plaza. The notable architectural features of this redwood-frame house are its large gothic windows and carved ornamental eaves. The general and his family lived here until 1890.

◆◆◆
SONOMA

Sonoma has a central plaza which was laid out by General Vallejo in 1835, surrounded by the largest collection of Mexican-era adobe buildings north of Monterey forming the **Sonoma State Historic Park**. Of prime importance is the San Francisco Solano Mission, founded in 1823. The padres' quarters in a long, low wing next to the present adobe church are Sonoma's most historic building (1825); the existing church dates from 1840. Also bordering the plaza is Vallejo's first home, Casa . Grande, built in 1836. The adobe Sonoma Barracks, built to house Mexican troops under

The padres' quarters at Sonoma, built only two years after the Mission was founded in 1823

general Vallejo's command, was the scene of the Bear Flag takeover in 1846. What is now the Toscano Hotel was an 1850s general store and library. Vasquez House, now a historical museum, was once the home of General Joseph Hooker, a Civil War general with a penchant for young girls of questionable virtue (hence the word 'hooker').

Sonoma is also famous for Sonoma Jack, a type of high-moisture cheese. It has been manufactured in Sonoma since 1931 and continues to be a traditional food item. 'Jack' cheeses were originally made on Monterey farms, pioneered by Scottish merchant, David Jacks. Nowadays, all flavours are available from onion or garlic to caraway and hot peppers.

WINERIES

Recommended vineyards in the Sonoma Valley with tours and tastings are:

Buena Vista (Sonoma) – California's oldest premium winery. Self-guided tours through the 1857 cellars, a tasting room with an antique press, and lovely grounds in which to picnic make this number one.

Chateau St Jean (Kenwood) – wines made here include the sparkling variety. Self-guided tours are available.

Gloria Ferrer Champagne Caves (Sonoma) – dedicated to sparkling wine, this vineyard has recently achieved more widespread recognition.

Gundlach-Bundschu (Sonoma) – visitors follow self-guided tours, but there are plenty of knowledgeable personnel around to give the answers. There is also a hiking trail with a view of the valley.

Sebastiani Vineyards (Sonoma) – a respected family winery with an award-winning product.

Russian River Wine Road recommendations are:

Clos du Bois (Healdsburg) – wines from the Alexander and Dry Creek valleys.

Foppiano Vineyards (Healdsburg) – family-owned since 1896.

Johnsons's Alexander Valley (Healdsburg) – unique tasting room contains a 1920s theatre pipe organ.
Korbel Champagne Cellars (Guerneville) – famous champagne cellars.
Simi (Healdsburg) – noted for its state-of-the-art equipment.
Sotoyome (Healdsburg) – the name is derived from the Old Rancho Sotoyome; where there were once ranches is now the heart of the county's wine country.

Accommodation

The Sonoma Valley and Russian River region is scattered with inns and bed and breakfast establishments. Among them are:
Camellia Inn, 211 North St, Healdsburg (tel: (707) 433 8182). An Italianate Victorian mansion furnished with antiques, twin marble fireplaces and an impressively ornate mahogany dining room.
Campbell Ranch Inn, 1475 Canyon Rd, Geyserville (tel: (707) 857 3476). Set in 35 acres (14 hectares) on top of a hill with vineyard views, this inn's five comfortable guest rooms feature king-size beds.
Sonoma Valley Inn, 550 2nd St W, Sonoma (tel: (707) 938 9200). More of a hotel with 75 rooms, and your choice of wood-burning fireplaces or private jacuzzis, plus kitchenettes.
Vintner's Inn, 4350 Barnes Rd, Santa Rosa (tel: (707) 575 7350). A 44-room country inn surrounded by a vineyard.

Restaurants

'**Depot 1870**', 241 1st St, West Sonoma (tel: (707) 938 2980) – a country inn with an inexpensive North Italian menu and a wine list that highlights local wineries.
John Ash and Co, 4350 Barnes Rd, Santa Rosa (tel: (707) 575 7350). One of California's great restaurants featuring the innovative wine-country cuisine of chef John Ash.
Kenwood, 9900 Sonoma Highway, Kenwood (tel: (707) 833 6326). Delicious, wine-country cuisine is served at lunch and dinner, surrounded by vineyards of the Sonoma Valley.
The Sonoma Cheese Factory, 2 Spain St, Sonoma (tel: (707) 996 1931) – a great place for lunch – sandwiches and salads feature all kinds of Sonoma Jack cheese. You can also watch this cheese being made and buy some to take out.

Shopping

A fun place to shop is the historic **Railroad Square** in Santa Rosa. Here there are two square blocks of curio shops, antique stores and restaurants. Also in Santa Rosa you'll find speciality shops in **Montgomery Village**.
In Healdsburg, stroll through the Plaza and adjoining streets. Fashions for women and children are the main feature of Sonoma's newest shopping area – **Red Lion Plaza** at Rohnert Park. There are some interesting boutiques in Petaluma's downtown historic district, Sebastopol, Guerneville and Duncan Mills, and plenty more shops in **Sonoma Plaza** in Sonoma itself.

WHAT TO SEE ELSEWHERE IN CALIFORNIA

'Great Moments of US History' – a Disneyland interpretation

◆◆◆
ANAHEIM ✓

The prime reason for coming to Anaheim is because it is a centre of major family attractions (including Disneyland).

Anaheim means 'home by the river' in German, and was given by settlers who came here with vine cuttings in 1857 – until the late 1800s this was the state's wine capital. When a blight devastated the vineyards, the grape growers turned to oranges, but it was Walt Disney's choice of the site for a new and different theme park that made Anaheim bloom. The city literally grew up around the 76 acres (31 hectares) of Magic Kingdom, and it is now Orange County's largest city. Anaheim's buildings are impressive, no more so than

the **Convention Center**, which not only caters to business people but frequently stages concerts, ice shows, etc. Also impressive is the **Stadium**. It cost $21 million to build, seats 70,000, and is the local home of the California Angels baseball and Ram's football teams. Guided tours available.

Then there are the shops – in modern multi-storey centres of cleverly designed villagey complexes. Try the Anaheim Plaza or Seaports of the Pacific at the Disneyland Hotel. The latter features waterfront restaurants and live country music on the wharf, an international bazaar, an off-road raceway, a video games centre and variety shows like the Polynesian Fantasy and Dancing Waters.

Nor does the city lack places to

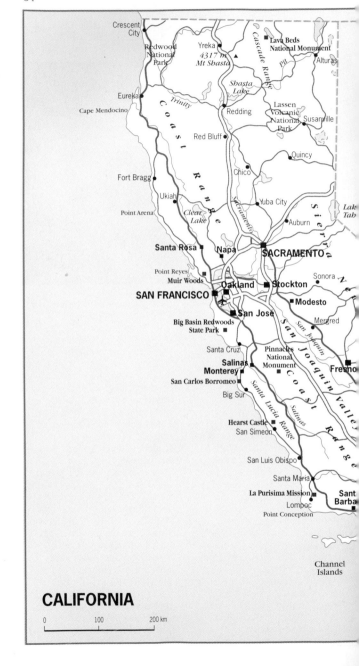

CALIFORNIA

0   100   200 km

UTAH

NEVADA

Mono Lake
Yosemite National Park
Devil's Postpile
Bishop
Scotty's Castle
Kings Canyon National Park
Ubehebe Crater
Independence
4418 m ▲ Mt Whitney
Sequoia National Park
Devil's Golf Course
Death Valley
Visalia
▲ 3368m
Delamo
Bakersfield
Ridgecrest
M o j a v e
Ghost Town of Calico
Lancaster
Barstow
Needle
D e s e r t
S o n o r a
Six Flags
Magic Mountain
Ventura
Desert
Pasadena
San Bernardino
ARIZONA
Oxnard
LOS ANGELES
Anaheim
Palm Springs
Long Beach Disneyland
Blythe
Salton Sea
Oceanside
Mt Palmer
Escondido
Brawley
SAN DIEGO
Colorado

MEXICO

ELSEWHERE IN CALIFORNIA

stay, suited to family budgets. Many are at the edge of **Disneyland** and this, of course, is the attraction that adults and children alike want to see. Since the park opened in 1955, it has never looked back, adding new shows and rides all the time. The lands are still 'themed' – Adventureland, Critter Country, Fantasyland, Frontierland, Main Street USA, Mickey's Toontown, New Orleans Square and Tomorrowland – each with its own special enticements. Mickey's Toontown, added in 1993, is the latest 'land' in 20 years. It is a whimsical recreation of Disney's most famous characters' homes. Favourite rides, such as 'Pirates of the Caribbean', 'Haunted Mansion', 'Jungle Cruise', 'Matterhorn Bobsleds' and 'Space Mountain', continue to operate, and there is constant live entertainment. 'Splash Mountain' features one of the world's longest and fastest flume drops – over 50ft (15m) high and reaching 40mph (64kph), as well as 100 'audio animatronic' characters which tell the story of *Song of the South*. Opened in 1995 is the 'Indiana Jones Adventure', featuring a harrowing journey through the ancient ruins of the Temple of the Forbidden Eye. One admission fee covers all (open until midnight at weekends and holidays).

A far cry from fruit-growing – Knott's Berry Farm

While in the Anaheim area you should combine a visit to Disneyland with the nearby attractions of the town of **Buena Park**. The most notable theme park here is **Knott's Berry Farm**, a success story bar none. Walter and Cordelia Knott came to Orange County in 1920 from San Luis Obispo (where they had been sharecroppers) and started a berry farm on 20 acres (8 hectares) of land. They sold fruit and jams from a roadside stand and later, chicken dinners. Today, the complex covers 150 acres (61 hectares) and features a wide range of rides and entertainments. The six themed areas are Ghost Town, Fiesta Village, Roaring 20's, Camp Snoopy, Indian Trail and Wild Water and popular rides include the 'Calico Mine Trip', 'Sky Jump' and 'Mystery Lodge'. The latest ride is 'Jaguar', one of the longest and scariest roller coaster rides in California. One entrance fee pays for all. One block from the park, at Beach Boulevard, **Medieval Times Dinner and Tournament** offers medieval banquets, while in Buena Park is **Wild Bill's Western Dinner Extravaganza**, a Western-themed dinner theatre.

◆
BORREGO SPRINGS
This desert oasis, 90 miles (145km) northeast of San Diego, is the best base for visiting the **Anza-Borrego Desert State Park** since it boasts plenty of motels in all price brackets. Most of the park's 600,000 acres (242,800 hectares) are as rugged as they were in Spanish times, so ranger guided walks or tours are recommended. From Borrego Springs itself, it is possible to take a 40-mile (64km) circular trip, stopping at Font's Point to look at the Badlands with its chasm gashed from towering granite walls, and at Palm Canyon where hundreds of palms grow.

◆◆◆
CARMEL ✓

Carmel is really little more than a village by the sea, albeit a charming arty one. Named by the Spanish in honour of the Carmelite friars, it is situated at the southern entrance point to the scenic **17 Mile Drive** (see **Monterey**, pages 93–4) and popular with honeymooners. You won't find skyscrapers or convention hotels here, accommodation is usually an inn and restaurants are cosily intimate. Shops, too, tend to be of the boutique, speciality and art gallery kind. Set on its sandy crescent on the Monterey Peninsula, backed by cypress-covered hills, Carmel is reminiscent of European coastal resorts.

Two miles (3 km) along the coast, **Point Lobos** was what Robert Louis Stevenson called 'the most beautiful meeting of land and sea on earth'. It is a pleasure to walk through this state reserve and possibly swim in a cove sheltered by Monterey cypress.

◆
CATALINA ISLAND

Situated 26 miles (42km) off the coast from Long Beach, this resort island used to be the property of William Wrigley Jr. It is noted for clear water and warm sandy beaches, appealing to sunbathers and snorkelers alike. From the pleasure pier at Avalon, the capital, glass-bottomed boats and flying-fish boats leave on tour. Public transport operates to the island's interior, but no cars are allowed on the island making hiking and cycling popular. Those who wish to stay here have a choice of resort hotels and inns, including the last home of novelist Zane Grey (now a guest house), and the Wrigley Mansion. Catalina can also easily be reached as a day's excursion from Long Beach by boat, hydrofoil or helicopter.

Ubehebe Crater is one of many extraordinary landforms in Death Valley, which was once the floor of an inland sea

◆◆◆
DEATH VALLEY

Adjoining Nevada, Death Valley National Park is America's third largest, covering 3,000 square miles (7,770 sq km), and contains the hottest spot in the US. During the Gold Rush, a party of prospectors (the 'forty-niners') were stuck in this hot, low, dry place, hence the valley's name, but there are springs and streams here and there is life: the pupfish (or desert sardine) has learnt to live and flourish in high temperatures. So do desert mammals and reptiles. And though Death Valley isn't green, it has plenty of other colours – Golden Canyon shines gold in the rising and setting sun; Mustard Canyon is ochre tinted; Mosaic Canyon's grey rocks contain pebbles in many different hues; and Red Cathedral, a natural clay amphitheatre, is indeed red. Take Artists' Palette Drive to enjoy some of the best of this colour.

The highlight is Dante's View, 5,474ft (1,668m) above sea-level, a point from which you can see almost all of Death Valley. Below is Badwater, 282ft (86m) below sea-level, and the lowest point in the US. Above are the Panamint Mountains and the Telescope Peak, over 11,000ft (3,000m) high. And in the distance, the second highest point in the United States, Mount Whitney, shimmers under its 14,494ft (4,417m) high snowcap. Nature's oddities abound in Death Valley, once the floor of an inland sea, as you can tell from sections of sand dunes. A bed of salt crystals is also evidence of the place's maritime past – an area of odd salt formations which remained after the sea evaporated have been named 'Gnome's Workshop'. There are man-made oddities, too, like the ghost town of Skidoo, once a mining centre, or Scotty's Castle, an unfinished Spanish-Moorish palace built in a remote canyon by flamboyant Californian, Walter Scott. Because of its temperatures, Death Valley's main tourist season is from mid-autumn to mid-spring.

◆
FRESNO

This lively city is the banking, financial and agricultural centre of the San Joaquin Valley. Almost right in the middle of California, it provides plenty to see and do and plenty of hotel chain accommodation. One of its focal points is **Roeding Park** where 157 acres (63 hectares) are planted with a variety of trees and shrubs. The park is the setting for **Chaffee Zoological Gardens** – with over 700 animals and birds and a computer-operated reptile house. In the park you'll also find **Story Land**, a children's fantasy area, with picnic sites and fishing lakes (closed December and January and weekdays the rest of winter and spring).

Another city park for a summer day is **Woodward Park**, on the San Joaquin River, with its bird sanctuary, amphitheatre, children's playground and

Japanese garden.

Fresno has several worthwhile museums; **Discovery Center** is a favourite with all ages. Highlights of this hands-on science museum are the exhibits of whisper cones, laser phone, electronic sound tree and native Indian artefacts (closed Mondays). At the **Metropolitan Museum of Art, History and Science** you can see Old Masters, still-life and *trompe l'oeil* paintings (closed Mondays and Tuesdays).

◆
LAGUNA BEACH
A typically Californian beach town clad with palms and eucalyptus, Laguna (to the south of LA) takes its name from the word for lakes (it has two freshwater lagoons). The place is so picturesque, the atmosphere so leisurely, that it has always been an artists' colony. Not surprisingly, you'll find boutiques, craft shops, art galleries, festivals and art-related events here.

◆◆◆
LA JOLLA
It looks like the French Riviera, this jewel of a resort reached in a 15-minute drive north from San Diego. La Jolla's postcard prettiness (along with its weather) has attracted the artistic for many years.

The blue expanse of Lake Tahoe is fringed by three National Forests

The Indians called this place 'La hoya', meaning cave – several caves can be seen from the cliff-top overlooking the most popular swimming beach, La Jolla Cove. You can go into the largest cave if you wish, through the Cave Curiosity Shop at the northern end of the Coast Boulevard and down 133 steps.

La Jolla Cove appeals to skin-divers as it is part of the San Diego-La Jolla Underwater Park, an underwater conservation area, but only experienced divers are allowed to explore it. Winter migration of the whales is best seen from Whale Point. Water and marine life are more than just for fun in this resort, which is also a research centre, being the home of the Salk Institute and the **Scripps Institution of Oceanography**. At the latter there are 22 large tanks housing sea mammals, crustaceans, fish and plants. Antique teddy bears enjoy a Victorian setting in the **Teddy Bear Museum** on Cave Street (free).

There is motel accommodation here, but the inns are more atmospheric; there are also many cosy bars, pavement cafés and fine restaurants.

◆◆◆
LAKE TAHOE

Lake Tahoe has the distinction of being two-thirds in California and one-third in Nevada and is an excellent year-round resort area. This 12 by 22-mile (19 by 35-km) alpine lake was discovered by pioneer John Fremont in 1844 on his journey from Oregon to California. It was just as central to the migration of the native Washoe Indians before the Gold Rush fortune hunters came along.

For scenic beauty, you could not do better since Tahoe lies in a basin between the main Sierra Nevada and the eastern offshoot of the Carson range, surrounded by the national forests of Eldorado, Tahoe and Toiyabe.

The region boasts the finest accommodation and restaurants in the High Sierra – 100 eating places, 16,000 rooms. It also boasts an incredible amount of sunshine and an equally incredible amount of winter snow – nearly 18ft (5.5m). From spring to autumn, hiking, cycling, horse-back riding and ballooning are popular. In summer, sailing, water-skiing, rafting and fishing are ideal – you can rent a boat from one of the marinas or take a paddle-boat cruise that includes a meal. For winter skiers, Lake Tahoe is a West Coast paradise: the Tahoe Basin is renowned as a world-class downhill skiing destination, but in addition it has thousands of acres available for cross-country skiing. There are 212 ski lifts and tows. The **Lake Tahoe Visitor Center** on Taylor Creek will give you information about trails, flora and fauna. Artefacts from the region's earliest days are on display at the **Lake Tahoe Historical Society Museum** (open late May to early September) on Highway 50,

Volcanic Mount Lassen broods over a sparkling, lake-strewn landscape

and you can also get details of the self-guided car tour of 20 landmarks in the South Tahoe area here. Those who seek city lodging should head for South Lake Tahoe.

◆◆
LASSEN VOLCANIC NATIONAL PARK

Some say it is a miniature Yellowstone, this small national park located 47 miles (75km) east of Redding, off Highway 44 in northern California. Mount Lassen, after a long sleep, erupted 300 times between 1914 and 1917. This snow-covered dome at the southern tip of the Cascades is the focal point of the park but there are numerous other peaks here, 50 wilderness lakes and acres of forests. Mount Lassen's bbbling mud pools, hot ings, cinder cones and the

steamy holes known as fumeroles are an exciting reminder that it is still an active volcano, but the recent restful decades have turned this into a safe (though still adventurous) area for hikers and skiers. Headquarters for the park are in Mineral on State Highway 36. The area's county seat is at Susanville, and this could be a good accommodation base. The second largest natural lake located within California, Eagle Lake, is only 20 miles (32km) from the town, and is noted for its fishing and sailing possibilities.

Within the park, numerous hiking trails lead to the thermal area. The 2½ mile (4km) Lassen Peak Trail leads to the top but an easier way takes you to Bumpass Hell, which is the largest hot-springs area – Little Hot Springs, Big Boiler,

Steam Engine and the Sulphur Works are all nearby. The park's eastern section is the most rugged but it may be reached by pack-horse trips which leave from Summit Lake. The resort area is around Manzamota Lake (only open in summer) where there are campsites and lodges available for travellers.

◆
MAMMOTH LAKES
This four-season holiday area lies in a 9,000ft (2,700m) deep, lake-strewn basin below Mammoth Mountain. The town of Mammoth Lakes itself is a resort base for excursions into the area, with a range of places to dine and lodge. It is a convenient base for drives to Yosemite National Park, some 30 miles (48km) northwest, or Inyo National Forest, a little further to the east. Two local lakes of interest are Convict Lake and man-made Crowley Lake, stocked with fish. Rainbow Falls is the site where the San Joaquin River tumbles 140ft (42m) over lava ledges, and nearby Devil's Postpile National Monument, created 900,000 years ago by hot lava, has giant columns resembling organ pipes.

Mammoth Lakes is a challenging territory for hikers, backpackers and mountain climbers, but most of all attracts the skiers. The region is one of America's largest ski areas, offering one of the longest seasons, sometimes as far into the year as July! You'll find 30 lifts, 150 trails, 30,000ft (9,000m) of vertical runs, cross-country

skiing, ice-skating on Convict Lake and wind-skiing in the meadows – and plenty of mountain lodges, too.

◆◆
MENDOCINO
Often called the 'New England of the West Coast', this village in northern California is favoured by artists and is frequently used as a location for films and television shows. Its Cape Cod style of architecture is due to the timber men who settled here from Maine in the mid-19th century. In addition to the quaint houses, some of which have been converted to bed and breakfast inns, there are unusual shops and art galleries, and cosy restaurants. The Mendocino coast, stretching from the Gualala River to Point No Pass, is a most attractive one, a draw for artists, fishermen and wine-growers. Along the southern part of Highway 1, several picturesque coastal villages are located, including Anchor Bay, Little River, Albion and Point Arena.

◆◆◆
MONTEREY
This scenic port is a must on anyone's itinerary. When Sebastian Vizcaino set foot on the Monterey Peninsula in 1602, its destiny was sealed – Monterey became one of the first and most successful settlements in California; indeed it was the capital until the American flag was raised in 1846.

Always dependent upon the sea, for a long time Monterey

was a whalers' retreat.
Fisherman's Wharf, built in 1848, served as a pier for trading schooners from around the Horn, and was the focal point for the whaling and subsequent sardine industries. Today, it is a tourist's delight, lined with seafood restaurants and speciality shops and departure point for whale-watching cruises.

More shops and restaurants are found along **Cannery Row**, whose renaissance is due to the fame of John Steinbeck's book *Cannery Row*. Between 1921 and 1946, Monterey was a sardine capital, with 16 canneries packing over 240,000 tons of sardines each year. When the sardines disappeared, the 'Row', as Steinbeck knew it, died; tourism reviving the area only in later years.

At the western end of the Row, the **Monterey Bay Aquarium** allows close-up viewing of the Bay's underwater world. The 177,000-sq-ft (16,000 sq m) aquarium provides homes for over 6,500 sea creatures from sharks to otters. Then there's the 28ft (8.5m) deep tank through which you can see a functioning kelp forest, and another tank which recreates the deep reefs and contains sharks, bat rays and other open-ocean fish.

Eight of Monterey's 19th-century buildings have been incorporated in **Monterey State Historic Park**. The old Custom House, for example, is the state's oldest government building, and California's first theatre was built here, adobe-style, as a boarding house and saloon.

Although the city is not neon-lit, it is lively, with a highly regarded September jazz festival and 70 other annual special events taking place within the Peninsula. There are plenty of hotels and golf courses, but perhaps the greatest attraction is the **17-Mile Drive** (see also **Carmel**, page 87). This scenic route takes you around the Peninsula from Pacific Grove to Carmel's Mission and back to Monterey, passing Seal Rock, Cypress Point, Spyglass Hill and Pebble Beach. There is a charge per car.

The Pacific coast near Monterey

◆◆
MOUNT PALOMAR

From the visitor's gallery in **Palomar Observatory**, you can view the huge telescope, which has a range of one billion (US) light-years. It utilises mirrors instead of a lens and therefore acts as a giant camera – photographs taken from it are on display in the exhibit hall. Mount Palomar is 40 miles (64m) northeast of San Diego.

◆
OAKLAND

From San Francisco, the bridge is more obvious than the community of Oakland, despite the fact that the latter is the Bay's largest rail and port city.

The Oakland–San Francisco Bay Bridge is an engineering marvel, spanning 8½ miles (14m) between Rincon Hill in San Francisco and the toll plaza in Oakland. At some point you are almost bound to cross it. The city of Oakland is, of course, commuter territory, but it is also the site of an enormous saltwater tidal lake – **Lake Merritt**. Canoe or row on it, jog or cycle around it – the lake is also a national duck refuge. At the northern end of Lakeside Park, **Children's Fairyland** has replicas of favourite nursery rhymes, some with live pets – a theme area said to have inspired Walt Disney for his own park. The **Oakland Museum of California**, on Oak and 10th Streets, documents the State's history, natural sciences and art. Closed Mondays and Tuesdays. At the foot of Broadway on Oakland Estuary, **Jack London's Waterfront** is the best place for food and entertainment. The author frequented Heingold's First and Last Chance Saloon here, now a restored attraction on the square. The Village, next door, is a themed shopping area.

◆
PETALUMA

You may well pass through this little town that held the title 'Egg Basket of the World' (it once produced a vast amount of eggs and poultry) on your way to or from Napa and Sonoma's wine country. If you can't resist oddities, stop – you'll like it. Petaluma trivia, for example, tells us it is the only town in North America with a commercial snail ranch; that the world's first and only drug store for chickens was located here; and that Winners' Circle Ranch, breeder of horses under 32 inches (81cm) high, is the only miniature horse farm west of the Mississippi open to the public!

All that apart, you may care to wander around the downtown historic buildings, some of them of typical Victorian style. They were designed with iron fronts in the belief that this would prevent fire. It didn't, but 26 of the old buildings do survive. On the outskirts of town, **Petaluma Adobe State Historic Park** contains California's largest adobe structure – General Vallejo's ranch of the 1840s.

◆◆
REDWOOD NATIONAL PARK

Within this national park, right in the north of California, are three state parks: Jedediah Smith Redwoods, Del Norte Coast and Prairie Creek Redwoods. In the **Jedediah Smith Redwoods State Park**, there are 19 memorial redwood groves, including the Frank Stout grove whose 340ft (104m) Stout Tree is the greatest attraction. Camping facilities and a beach can be found along the Smith River. There are several campsites in various sections of the **Del Norte Coast State Park** and, of the trails which lead from them, the 2-mile (3km) Trestle Loop Trail behind the Red Alder camping ground, is thought to be best. **Prairie**

Creek Redwoods State Park has a host of redwoods and, thanks to generous rainfall, is green with other foliage besides, so that Fern Canyon's walls are emerald with mosses and lichens. Herds of elk are visible in the meadows of the Madison Grant section of this park and the best trail is said to be Revelation.

A shuttle bus service operates from the visitor centre in Orick to Tall Trees Grove, where the tallest known tree, Libby Tree, is over 368ft (112m).

◆
RIVERSIDE

In earlier days this city, in inland southern California, was a rich centre for navel oranges – in 1895 there were 20,000 acres (8,000 hectares) of them. Reminders of that early wealth remain visible in its elaborate Victorian architecture.

Heritage House is a particularly fine example, built in 1891 at a cost of $10,000, and beautifully restored. Another landmark is **Mission Inn**, originally a 12-room adobe structure of 1875, now a deluxe hotel containing over a million dollars' worth of antiques (tours of the hotel by the public are possible). Opposite the old City Hall, the Renaissance-style **Municipal Museum** (closed Mondays) houses Indian artefacts and exhibits of the citrus industry's early days. Further reminders of those days is contained in the **California Citrus State Historic Park**, an area of recreated turn-of-the-century buildings and orange groves.

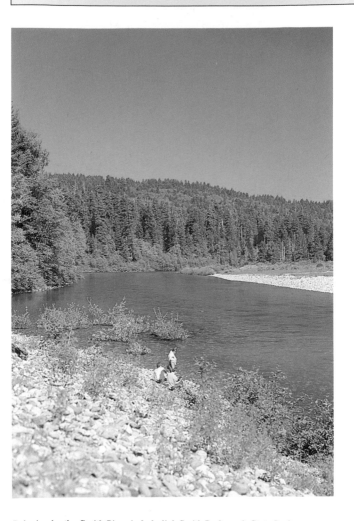

Relaxing by the Smith River in Jedediah Smith Redwoods State Park

Agricultural traditions are kept alive at the **Riverside Botanical Gardens** (free), 37 acres (15 hectares) of hilly terrain whose emphasis is on dry-climate plants – over 3,000 species.

For the children, **Castle Amusement Park** is a 27-acre (11-hectare) family park whose focal point is a three-level arcade crammed with games.

◆◆
SACRAMENTO

California's state capital has
something for everyone: history,
waterfront activity, elegant
restaurants. It started to grow
when Swiss-born John Sutter
built a fort at the confluence of
the American and Sacramento
Rivers in 1839. Today, the
restored structure is **Sutter's
Fort State Historic Park** and it
shows how things looked when
this was central California's first
outpost of civilisation. On
special Living History days,
guides in period costume re-
enact life as it was in the 1840s.
Adjacent, the **State Indian
Museum** displays aspects of
Indian life and culture.

Old Sacramento, along the
Sacramento River, comprises
28 acres (11 hectares) of Gold
Rush era buildings,
cobblestone streets and
wooden pavements, where one
can take a trip back in time the
easy way. This is how the area
looked in the 1850's to 1870's,
though there wouldn't have
been the cafés and restaurants,
boutiques and gift shops that
you'll find here now. Among
the restored structures are a
one-room school, an assay
office, a post office and the
Eagle Theatre, a reconstruction
of the West Coast's first theatre
which stages shows. Ardent
train spotters will find a
comprehensive railway
museum in Old Sacramento –
the **California State Railroad
Museum** features 21
locomotives and innumerable
historic railway relics. Most
famous is the *Southern Pacific
4294* steam locomotive,

*Sacramento's elegant State Capital
dates from the 1860's*

weighing over a million pounds
(453,600 kilos). Others to look
for include Lucius Beebe's
lavish private travelling rail car
and the 1860s *Governor
Stanford* steam locomotive.
Steam rides are available in
summer. Sacramento used to
be the end of the line for the
Pony Express. This western
terminus, now the **B F Hastings
Building** (free), shows exhibits
of this special delivery service.
Gold is the highlight display at
the **Discovery Museum**
(closed Mondays, except
holidays), a reconstructed
version of the 1854 City Hall
and Waterworks building. Nor
has Old Sacramento's

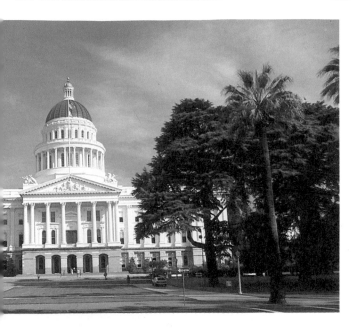

waterfront been forgotten. It was a busy supply centre in the 1850s with hundreds of paddle-wheelers, like the *Delta King* (now permanently docked and a hotel, restaurant, saloon and theatre), plying their trade along the river. Enjoy the experience on a replica paddle-wheeler, such as the *Matthew McKinley*, one of several to offer daily cruises. Not far from the Old Sacramento sector, **Governor's Mansion** has been home to 13 state governors, including Ronald Reagan. It's open now as a State Historic Park and showplace of 19th-century opulence. The West's oldest art museum, the **Crocker Art Museum** (closed Mondays and Tuesdays), is located on O Street and is most noted for a major collection of Old Master drawings.

For pure recreation, take to the rivers – both the Sacramento and American can be fished or rafted. Youngsters will find a children's themed area, playground and amusement centre as well as the city's **Zoo** in **William Land Park**, or you could take them along to **Gibson Ranch County Park**, in existence since the 1870s, where they are free to feed the domestic animals. If they're very energetic, head for **Waterworld USA** (open late May to early September) on Exposition Boulevard – 14 acres (6 hectares) of wet and wild attractions, including high-speed slides and activity pools.

ELSEWHERE IN CALIFORNIA

◆
SALINAS

In the heart of a productive farming belt, a 20-minute drive from Monterey, Salinas was John Steinbeck's birthplace. His house, currently a restaurant and gift shop, is part of what has been designated **Old Town** – nine square blocks in the heart of downtown. Some of his original manuscripts and other memorabilia can be seen in the nearby **John Steinbeck Library**. His Salinas experiences led to such novels as *East of Eden* and *Of Mice and Men*.

◆
SAN JOSÉ

From 1849 to 1851, San José was the state capital, but the 20th-century claim of this city to the south of San Francisco is as a leading centre for technology. Microchips apart, the most bizarre place to visit is the **Winchester Mystery House**. Eccentric Sarah Winchester (heiress to the famous rifle fortune) was so convinced that she would live as long as she kept adding to her mansion, that carpenters were busy for 38 years installing windows, doors (often opening onto walls), fireplaces and staircases (often leading to nowhere). She couldn't keep the spirits at bay, but the eerie 4-storey, 160-room house is worth the tour price. Visitors can guide themselves around the gardens and outbuildings, and can also see the **Winchester Historic Firearms** and **Antique Products Museums**.

◆◆
SAN JUAN CAPISTRANO

This city, between Los Angeles and San Diego, is most famous for its **Mission San Juan Capistrano**, founded in 1776 and the seventh in the chain established by Father Serra. Take yourself round the Serra Chapel and the ruins of the original church, to which it is said the famous swallows return each year on 19 March. The city which has grown round the Mission, has become a popular resort readily accessible to Disneyland. Situated on rolling hills between the mountains and the sea, San Juan Capistrano is filled with lovely old adobe buildings and has an Amtrak terminal that is a restored 1895 Santa Fe railway station.

◆◆◆
SAN SIMEON ✓

A crowning glory – or is it folly – of the Central Coast is Hearst Castle or, as it has since become, **Hearst San Simeon State Historical Monument**. It was the 'fantasy' estate of newspaper magnate William Randolph Hearst, born into a wealthy San Francisco family and given his own newspaper to run when aged only 24. He was the man who said 'Pleasure is worth what you can afford to pay for it'. San Simeon glitters atop a knoll overlooking that great scenic route, Highway 1. 'La Cuesta Encantada' or the Enchanted Hill was where

A tycoon's dream come true – Hearst Castle at San Simeon

Hearst entertained people from all walks of life. His family donated the estate to California in 1957, 6 years after his death. The man who expanded his business into a vast publishing empire collected *objects d'art* from around the world to fill his 'castle', a combination of Italian, Spanish, Moorish and French architecture that took nearly 30 years to complete. Inside there are life-size statues of saints, 16th-century silk banners, priceless tapestries and marble medallions, each weighing a ton. Outside, there are sculpture gardens, pools and marble terraces. Because the estate is so big – comprising 123 acres (50 hectares) of grounds – visitors have the choice of three separate tours of the house, plus a garden tour from April to October (advance reservations recommended).

◆
SANTA ANA

The government seat of Orange County, Santa Ana may be reached from Los Angeles via the Santa Ana Freeway and is a good base for touring the county. Its own major tourist attraction is the **Bowers Museum** (closed Mondays), a hacienda-style structure that houses an outstanding and very large collection of West Coast Indian and pre-Columbian art. Part of the museum is the **Kidseum**, an interactive centre where children learn about the history of several cultures through story-telling, puppet shows and handicrafts.

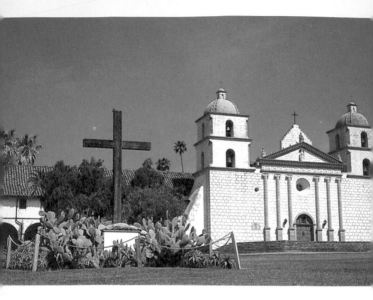

◆◆
SANTA BARBARA

This is a famous Spanish-influenced beach resort with distinctive red-tile-roofed buildings. A 1925 law has helped preserve Santa Barbara's historic legacy and many of its fine old structures have been lovingly restored. One of those is the **County Courthouse**. It takes up a whole city block and is considered one of the greatest public buildings in the West. Inside, there are handpainted frescos, wrought-iron chandeliers, historic exhibits and Tunisian tiles; outside, a sculptured façade and sunken gardens. From its 70ft (21m) clock-tower you can see across the city. Free guided tours some days. The courthouse is a key site along what Santa Barbara calls

The 'Queen of Missions' at Santa Barbara was founded in 1786

its 'Red Tile Tour', which will also take you past **El Presidio de Santa Barbara State Historic Park** (free). The guard's house and Canedo Adobe are part of the original Spanish fort on a site blessed by Father Serra in 1782, but the padre's quarters and chapels are reconstructions. It was Spanish conquistador, Sebastian Vizcaino who sailed into Santa Barbara's bay in 1602 and named the port after the saint whose birthday it was that day. By 1786, the presidio was the focal point of the Spanish stronghold whose **Mission Santa Barbara** was so beautiful it was called 'Queen of Missions'.

In August, you will see the

Plaza de la Guerra turned into a colourful market-place for the annual celebration of the Old Spanish Days Fiesta. El Paseo's shopping arcade, built around the Guerra family's 1827 adobe home, is redolent of Spain with its speciality shops, art galleries and dining courtyard. Another fine place to shop and eat is Stearns Wharf at the foot of State Street; from here you can overlook miles of beaches. Treasures from this historic city's past are on view in the **Historical Museum and Covarrubias Adobe** (closed Mondays; free) on E de la Guerra Street, whilst much of the display area of the **Santa Barbara Museum of Natural History** on Puesta del Sol Road is devoted to native Indian artefacts. Also in the vicinity, in an area bounded by Mission Creek, is an observatory and planetarium. The beach – and there are 30 miles (48km) of it – is still the number one reason for selecting Santa Barbara as a base. There are also family-priced motels and opportunities for most watersports.

To the north of town, along Highway 154, vineyards produce premier Californian wines – you can taste them at several establishments.

◆
SANTA CRUZ

Santa Cruz is a seaside resort 90 minutes' drive south from San Francisco, whose 1904 boardwalk or promenade was the first attraction of its kind on the West Coast. The **Beach Boardwalk** has since been rebuilt, but its amusement park, arcade of games and old-fashioned carousel continue to operate. On the municipal **Pier**, adjacent, you'll find a market, seafood restaurants and the departure point for bay cruise ferries. Abundant marine life can be seen in the nearby **Natural Bridges State Park** area which is noted for its sandstone arch. Not far from here, at the **Long Marine Laboratory and Marine Aquarium** (part of the University of California), there are tidepool aquariums, an 85ft (26m) skeleton of a blue whale and the chance to look in the back door at current research (closed Mondays). Regional natural history exhibits are displayed at the **Santa Cruz City Museum**, and in the octagonal landmark that was the Hall of Records and is now the **Santa Cruz County Historical Trust Museum**, county history is recorded in exhibits (both museums closed Mondays; free). More unusual is the **Santa Cruz Surfing Museum** inside a lighthouse (open Thursday to Monday, weather permitting).

Like the other coastal communities, Santa Cruz is big on watersports: pier fishing, sailing from the small yacht harbour, powered craft, and deep-sea fishing charters. A popular excursion will take you to Felton in the Santa Cruz mountains where a 1920s train will take you on a $2\frac{1}{2}$ hour trip from the redwoods at Roaring Camp back to Santa Cruz.

ELSEWHERE IN CALIFORNIA

◆◆
SEQUOIA AND KINGS CANYON NATIONAL PARKS

These adjacent parks form the gateway to the southern Sierras. Dominating the beauty of the natural scenery that stretches from the foothills of the San Joaquin Valley to the Sierra's crest, is Mount Whitney, the second highest mountain in the US – but the sequoias themselves are gargantuan enough. The road that circuits the southwestern corner is open year-round; the other only in summer. If you choose to drive, take the General's Highway, a 46-mile (74km) paved link between both parks, which passes the greatest examples of sequoias, all named after generals, the General Grant Tree, for example, is the second largest known living tree on earth at 267ft (81m) high and 107ft (33m) in circumference. But look also for the General Sherman Tree, 272ft (82m) high and 106ft (32m) round, the Robert E Lee Tree and the Hart Tree.

If you are hiking, take the Congress Trail Loop, which winds through several sequoia stands for 2 miles (3km), providing access to fishing areas, scenic outlooks and meadows. Seeing the parks this way, on foot – or by mule – is even more recommended than using wheels. Lodgepole Visitor Center is the starting point for guided hikes and backpack excursions, though there are other information centres at Grant and Cedar Groves.

Some of the better-known park attractions are Tunnel Log, where one of the fallen trees has created what looks like a doorway, Beadle Rock, a vantage point at sunset, and Moro Rock, from where you can see the Great Western Divide mountain range. Strange geographical formations are found in Crystal Cave – a park ranger will explain them. Relics on Hospital Rock relate to the Mono Indians, once the area's inhabitants. Another interesting sight is Tharp's Log, a log cabin in a hollow sequoia. It was used by explorer Hale Tharp.

Some say the greatest natural beauty is at Mineral King where there are sub-alpine meadows. The area may be reached 25 miles (40km) south of Three Rivers in Sequoia National Park. The least explored sections of Kings Canyon lie in the centre. Campsites (open all year) are scattered throughout both parks and there are stores and supply centres for obtaining provisions and fishing licences. Mules and horses may be hired from June to September at Giant Forest, Grant Grove, Cedar Grove, Mineral King and Owens Valley.

◆
SHASTA LAKE

This, the state's largest man-made lake, is a recreational area formed by the Shasta Dam which backs up the Sacramento, McCloud, Squaw and Pit Rivers in northern California. With 370 miles

(595km) of shoreline and a surface area of 30,000 acres (12,140 hectares), its watersport potential is one of the best. A few days on a houseboat, for instance, is one of the more unusual ways to enjoy the region. Other types of boat are available for rent and may indeed be necessary to reach some of the campsites maintained by the Forest Service.

Certainly the only way to reach Shasta Caverns is by boat. A ferry service operates year-round, 2 miles (3km) off Interstate 5, to take visitors across the lake. Tour buses on the other side are the transport for the short scenic trip up 800ft (240m) of mountainside to the caverns. They comprise a series of large connected caves where miniature waterfalls and countless stalactites and stalagmites have become a visual fairy-tale wonderland.

◆
SOLVANG
Does this sound like a Danish name? It is, for Solvang (meaning 'Sunny Valley') was founded by Danish settlers in 1911. This small town in Santa Ynez Valley north of Santa Barbara is pleasantly rural, its buildings and windmills featuring *bingingsvaerk* walls, typical of Danish hamlets in the Middle Ages. Many of the shops here sell Danish goods and its cafés serve Scandinavian cuisine. Tribute to northern roots is paid each September when a special festival brings out all those with

The General Sherman Tree in Sequoia National Park

Danish national costume. Two Solvang musts are a ride on a horse-drawn street car and a visit to **Santa Inés Mission** on the eastern outskirts of town. The peaceful Santa Ynez Valley serves as a city escape hatch. It is studded with horse farms and scenic parks of which the most popular is **Nojoqui Falls Park**, named after the 164ft (50m) falls.

◆
VENTURA
Both a mission town and seaside resort, Ventura is a good vacation base 70 miles (112km) northwest from Los Angeles. **Mission San Buenaventura** is in the centre of town – the ninth in the chain and the last to be founded by Father Serra. It is especially noted for lovely

gardens and an archaeological museum.

Sandy beaches, surfing and fishing areas give Ventura its sporting outlook. A scheduled boat service operates to the offshore Channel Islands National Park, and, 15 miles (24km) inland, the Ojai Valley offers numerous outdoor activities and cultural events.

◆◆◆
YOSEMITE ✓

Being the grandest and most splendid of California's national parks, Yosemite is a holiday area in its own right. Thanks to conservation campaigner, John Muir, it became the state's first park by Act of Congress in 1864. The focal point for the majority of holiday-makers is the 7 square miles (11 sq km) of meadow and forest that make up Yosemite Valley, where there are campsites and other lodgings and facilities. This is where you can shop for food, and rent a horse.

A summer sightseeing tour of Yosemite takes in the highest waterfall, Yosemite Falls. In summer one can take the winding road to panoramic Glacier Point or hike the Four Mile Trail, a steep, zig-zag descent to the valley floor. There are hiking trails in the park to suit both the novice and the expert, and short horse or mule trips can easily be arranged. However, trips to the back country do need a special permit (available from the ranger stations) and fishing the park's streams and rivers requires a licence. Gateway to the high country is Tuolumne, an alpine meadow with its own summer campsite and naturalist programmes. In winter most roads are closed but the main valley activity centre continues to operate and has its own outdoor skating rink at Curry Village.

Wintersport enthusiasts will find plenty of trails for cross-country skiing as well as downhill runs at Badger Pass. Ski equipment can be rented during the season which runs from around mid-December to early April.

Yosemite National Park, in the heart of the Sierra Nevada

PEACE AND QUIET

Countryside and Wildlife in California

by Paul Sterry

California is a strikingly beautiful state with one of the most varied terrains in the whole of North America. Although famous for its coastline, you can leave the Pacific, cross immense valleys to reach snow-capped mountains and finish up in barren deserts, all in a day! The marine life around the coast is rich and varied. Since the prevailing winds are from the west, the coastal lowlands have a mild climate with plenty of rainfall. However, in southern California, mountain ranges relieve the winds of most of their moisture, so the plains beyond them have become the parched Mojave and Colorado deserts. California's wildlife is as rich and varied as its terrain. Blue whales, the largest living animals, are sometimes seen offshore, and the world's largest living things, the giant sequoias, still persist in the Sierra Nevada. Over 400 species of bird have been recorded in the state.

The Coastline

Much of California's coast is rugged, beautiful and varied. The northern half is influenced by the cold Japanese current which sweeps down from Alaska as far as Point Conception, north of Los Angeles. Further south, the coastline swings sharply eastward, leaving the cold waters to swing away from the shore and warmer waters push up from the south. The north/south divide influences the wildlife as well as the climate. In the north, the coastal redwood thrives, particularly at Muir Woods to the north of San Francisco Bay. Though smaller than their giant relative, these trees are still impressive and inspiring. The coastline is dramatic and never more so than at Point Reyes National Seashore. Here, northern sea-lions bark in the surf and shorebirds such as black oystercatcher and willet feed on the beaches. To reach Point Reyes, head north from San Francisco on US 101 across the Golden Gate Bridge, exit on Highway 1 and after passing Bolinas Lagoon head to Olema and follow the signs off Highway 1 to the Point Reyes National Seashore Visitor Center. For Muir Woods National Monument cross the Golden Gate Bridge on US 101, exit on Highway 1 and follow signs. Pointe Vicente on the Palos Verde peninsula in Los Angeles is another good coastal spot, and the piers at Huntington Beach, Newport Beach and Corona del Mar are also worth visiting. They can be reached by heading south from Los Angeles and driving along the coastal Highway 1. It is always worth scanning out to sea, not only for seabirds but also for whales. California grey whales pass from November until March on their way to and from their breeding grounds in the lagoons of Baja California.

Marshes and Wetlands

Wetland areas occur throughout California from the coastal lagoons which attract waders at high tide, to the desert oases miles inland. The bottom of Central Valley, west of Enterprise, was at one time the winter haunt for tens of millions of wetland birds and, although drainage and agriculture have altered this forever, there are still areas protected from change. The Gray Lodge Waterfowl Area in Central Valley, for example, still attracts over a million ducks and geese in winter. The commonest ducks are pintail, American wigeon, lesser scaup and ruddy duck, but they can be joined by up to 15 other species, depending on the size and location of the water. Long-billed curlews haunt the marshy margins alongside American coots. This concentration of wildlife inevitably attracts a variety of predators such as red-tailed and the more unusual Swainson's hawks.

There are a surprising number of good wetland sites in and around many Californian towns and cities. The Andree Clark Bird Refuge is an excellent example; to reach it leave Highway 101 in Santa Barbara on Cabrillo Boulevard and turn right on to Los Patos Way. Harbor Lake Park on the Palos Verde peninsula in Los Angeles attracts ducks and gulls, but for even more variety, visit the marshes at Bolsa Chica, which is adjacent to Highway 1 near Huntington Beach. Look for gulls, waders, terns and egrets.

To get the best out of wetland birdwatching, it is useful to

Long-billed curlews often call loudly in flight

know a few 'tricks of the trade'. Ducks and waders are normally easy to see, but many of the smaller birds prefer to skulk in the bushes, their calls being the only thing which gives their presence away. The way to draw these secretive birds out into the open is to 'pish'. This technique, which only seems to work with American birds, involves making a series of abrupt hissing sounds through clenched teeth. A burst of short, high-pitched squeaks sometimes has a similar effect, and the National Audubon Society sells ready-made wooden squeakers for this very purpose. Try it anywhere and you will be amazed what pops out of the bushes!

Southern Mountains

Although they lack the grandeur of the Sierra Nevada further north, southern California can boast two major mountain ranges of its own. The Transverse Range runs east from Point Conception and holds the Santa Monica, San Gabriel and San Bernardino mountains, while the Peninsular Range, which runs south into Baja California, comprises the Santa Ana, Palomar and Laguna mountains.

The summit of Mount Pinos, nearly 9,000ft (2,700m) above sea-level, is as good a place as any to see the wildlife of the southern mountains. A road leads to a car park near the summit and from here the visitor can explore the surrounding area. Californian ground squirrels and grey squirrels are common and often

oblivious to people.

If you make the return trip down the mountain at dusk you stand a good chance of seeing some of the more unusual mammals. Bobcats, coyotes and mule deer all haunt the woodland and if you are really lucky you may see a black bear. Bears may look cuddly and friendly, but they are often unpredictable. If you do see one it is best to watch it from the safety of your car.

The largest bird likely to be seen is the golden eagle and patient observers often get very good views as the birds soar overhead. To reach Mount Picos head north from Los Angeles on Interstate 5 (Golden State Freeway). After Gorman, turn left to Frazier Park, fork left at the town of Lake of the Woods to the ranger station. The pass at Pine Cove and Idyllwild on Highway 243 is also good.

Deserts

Lying in the rainshadow of the southern mountains are California's eastern deserts – barren lands where rainfall is infrequent and erratic. Despite drought and heat, deserts hold a fascinating variety of specialised plants and animals. Although they grade into one another, the two major deserts are very different in character. To the north of the region, the Mojave Desert occupies land 1,000–4,000ft (330–1,000m) above sea-level, whereas to the south the Colorado Desert stretches from Salton to the Mexican border and lies at lower altitudes. Some areas of the desert are actually below

PEACE AND QUIET

Joshua trees are a characteristic feature of the Mojave Desert

sea-level, culminating in the fearful Death Valley which, at minus 282ft (86m), is the lowest point in North America. The Joshua Tree National Park, which lies across the San Andreas Fault, contains 872 square miles (2,258sq km) of both Mojave and Colorado Desert.

Joshua Tree

The name was coined by westward-trekking Mormons who thought they resembled Joshua at prayer. These imposing plants, which are a species of yucca and only occur here above an altitude of about 3,000ft (900m), are crucial to the survival of much desert life. They provide nesting sites for 25 species of birds, shade from the noon-day sun for mammals and lizards, and their flowers provide nectar for yucca moths.

Despite the lack of water, the deserts harbour many well-adapted mammals. Nocturnal species avoid the sun's rays, but pronghorn antelope and desert bighorn sheep seem indifferent to the heat. A night drive through the desert may reveal coyotes and desert kangaroo rats caught in the car's headlights. Kangaroo rats are endearing creatures which are seemingly fearless of man. Deserts are much favoured by reptiles. The desert iguana haunts the vicinity of creosote bushes in the low desert, and the chuckwalla, California's largest lizard, occurs around rocky outcrops.

The Living Desert Reserve in Palm Desert has nature trails and desert exhibits, and the Indian Reservation at Palm Canyon, south of Palm

Springs, is worth visiting.
Hummingbirds are attracted to
feeders here and there is plenty
of desert wildlife.

Salton Sea

Despite the fact that this lake is
effectively man-made, it is
frequented by vast numbers of
birds: half a million ducks
alone spend the winter here
and the flocks comprise up to
20 species. The margins of the
lake and the surrounding land
support up to 50,000
wintering geese including
Canada, snow and the rare
Ross' goose.

Almost any shorebird present
on the coast is likely to turn up
on the Salton Sea and up to six
species of heron and egret are
regularly seen. A careful
search of the flocks of birds
may even reveal the unusual
white-faced ibis, a speciality
of the area. Dead trees around
the edge of the lake provide
ideal perches for America's
national emblem, the bald
eagle, conspicuous with its
white head and white tail, and,
from July to September, the
Salton Sea also attracts birds
from Mexico such as wood
stork, blue-footed and brown
boobies and black skimmers.
The rough 'brush' country
surrounding the lake contains
typical dry-habitat animals.
The best place to observe the
Salton Sea is at the
headquarters of the National
Wildlife Refuge at the southern
end of the lake. To reach it,
drive north from Brawley on
Highway 111 and turn left into
Sinclair Road. A trail leads to the
water's edge.

Yosemite National Park

Yosemite is California's most
famous National Park and
contains well over 1,000
square miles (2,500 sq km) of
awe-inspiring scenery set in
the High Sierras. Immense
trees complement the grand
scale of the glaciated rock
formations which tower above
the central Yosemite Valley,
itself already 4,000ft (1,200m)
above sea-level.

Initial access to the park is
through Yosemite Valley, which
is dominated by two dramatic
rock formations so beloved of
rock climbers. El Capitan has a
sheer rock-face 3,500ft (1,066m)
high, and the famous Half
Dome rises 4,800ft (1,460m)
above the Tenaya Valley
below. Almost everything
about Yosemite is majestic,
including the 620ft (188m)-high
Bridalveil falls. Yosemite is
geared up for visitors. In the
summer months the valley floor
can be packed with people but,
as is the case with most
American parks, the number of
tourists drops off dramatically
after Labor Day. Even if the
park is crowded when you
visit, you can easily escape the
hordes by following one of the
numerous tracks or route-
marked trails. It is amazing
how few people stray further
than a few hundred yards from
information centres and car
parks. From the valley you can
easily reach the aptly named
Mirror Lake, in which flowering
dogwoods cast beautiful
reflections. The Tuolumne
Meadows, at 8,600ft (2,600m)
high, are red with the flowers
of the Indian paintbrush plant.

PEACE AND QUIET

Sequoia National Park

High in the Sierra Nevada lies the Sequoia National Park, 604 square miles (1,564 sq km) of land containing the deepest canyons in the state and the world's largest living trees. As a result of thoughtful planning, many hundreds of miles of trails have been laid out for hikers, and some of North America's highest mountains can be seen from ridges in the park. For the first-time visitor, the scale of the scenery and trees will take the breath away.

The Largest Living Things

Giant sequoias, *Sequoiadendron giganteum*, were once widespread across North America. However, the Ice Age wiped out most of their kind and they are now restricted to high altitudes in the Sierra Nevada. Sequoia and nearby Kings Canyon National Parks are the two most accessible places to see these giants.

Giant sequoias (also confusingly known as redwoods but a different species to the tall coastal redwoods) are not only the largest living things in the world but are also among the oldest. Many individuals are thought to be over 2,000 years old and are second only, in terms of age, to the bristlecone pine, a relict population of which is found in the nearby White Mountain range (see page 114).

As in Yosemite National Park, mule deer, squirrels, chipmunks and black bear are frequently seen or heard. Black bears can be troublesome and noisy nocturnal visitors to campsites; campers are advised not to keep food in their tents! Sadly, it was in this park that the last wild grizzly bear in California was seen, all the others had been hunted to extinction and this female was thought to have died after a solitary old age. The headquarters for Sequoia and Kings Canyon National Parks is at Ash Mountain. Drive east from Visalia on State 198 and collect maps and information from the interpretive centre.

Mono Lake

A visit to Mono Lake, set in the sagebrush of the Great Basin of California, and with its extraordinary moon-like landscape, is a unique experience. The waters of the lake support a wealth of specialised wildlife which contrasts markedly with the animals and plants of the surrounding desert.

The bizarre pinnacles and platforms which line the margins of Mono Lake are composed of a substance called tufa. These formations are similar in appearance and structure to stalagmites, being composed of the same chemical, calcium carbonate. The lake is the site of considerable environmental controversy. The waters of the Lee Vining River which once fed it have now been diverted to quench the thirst of the city of Los Angeles and, not surprisingly, this has caused a distinct drop in the water level of the lake. This is not only exposing more and more tufa

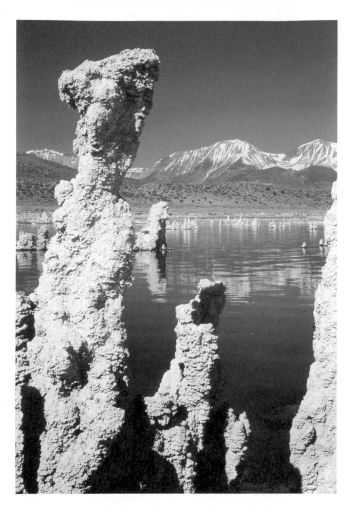

Strange white pillars made of tufa (calcium carbonate) line the margins of Mono Lake

to the erosion of wind and rain, but it is also threatening several species of nesting birds. A quarter of California's breeding population of California gull breed on Negit Island and the black-necked grebes are also at risk and only prompt action will help them.

PEACE AND QUIET

Bristlecone pines are thought to be the oldest living things

The Oldest Living Things

High in the White Mountains of California grow the bristlecone pines, some of the oldest living things on the planet. It is extraordinary to think that many of these trees were already mature before the birth of Christ. Many of the ancient bristlecone pines are thought to be over 3,000 years old, and at least one is considered to be approaching its 4,000th birthday – an awe-inspiring contrast to the modern US! The Shulman Grove, just beyond the Westguard Pass, is an easily accessible point to see the trees and, as you might expect, at nearly 10,000ft (3,000m) above sea-level, the scenery and views around the pines are spectacular. Birds of prey soar on thermals, mountain chickadees and pygmy nuthatches feed in the trees, and calliope hummingbirds somehow manage to survive up here. Lying in the rainshadow of the Sierra Nevada, there is much less rainfall in the White Mountains than in the Sierras to the west. As a result, the air is dry and clear and you can see for miles.

American Avocet

This is one of the most attractive of North America's wading birds. It has striking black and white wings and back, and white underparts. In the breeding season, the head and neck have an orange-buff wash, a characteristic which is shared by juvenile birds. American avocets have long, bluish legs, but the most striking feature is the long, upturned bill. When feeding, this is used to sift small water creatures from water and shallow mud. American avocets are often seen in small flocks and can be observed on marshes and lakes such as Salton Sea, Mono Lake and on many coastal wetlands.

FOOD AND DRINK

California spells fruit – and more fruit. Where groves of orange trees once stood is now the site of Disneyland, but there are still countless orchards for citrus fruits, peaches, avocados, dates and walnuts. They grow mostly in the south where the weather is good year-round. Fruits may be bought freshly at farmers' markets.

California also spells seafood – and more seafood. Fat shrimp, crab, abalone, swordfish, fresh tuna, red snapper – these and other delicacies are on the menus of California's restaurants. One of the best places to go for lunch is San Francisco's waterfront where seafood may be bought by the carton.

Mexico has exerted a strong influence on Californian cuisine. *Guacamole* and *tomales* are not only generally available but are also authentic in every part of the state, most especially in San Diego.

Of all the other ethnic groups who have brought their culinary talents to Californian kitchens, the Orientals have probably had most influence. The original Trader Vic's opened in San Francisco and no one should miss eating out at one of this city's Chinatown restaurants.

Steaks and prime rib are still an important part of any menu out West – going back to the days when enormous cattle ranches gave California its most important industry. Salad to accompany the meal is always welcome, and Californian salads are excellent (try the famous Green Goddess dressing which was invented in San Francisco). Other local specialities include *cioppino*, a soup cum stew made from seafood, and San Francisco's sourdough bread. Martini, too, is associated with the area (it is said to have first been concocted in San Francisco). But perhaps the area's best-known speciality is its wine. The Napa and Sonoma Valleys, north of San Francisco, are the most famous for wine and it is easy for tourists with a hired car to travel along the 'wine roads'. One of the earliest vineyards of note was Buena Vista in Sonoma County, founded by a Hungarian. Nowadays, there are many more vineyards to visit in the Sonoma Valley, including Sebastiani and Glen Ellen. Most of them offer tours and tastings, as indeed do those wineries located in the Napa Valley. Here, you'll find Beringer, Charles Krug and Rutherford Hill. Not content with the familiar tried and tested, California's innovative and promotional streak brought both the 'blush' wine (a very pale *rosé* made with zinfandel grapes) and the wine cooler (a light wine and fruit mixture) to widespread attention.

Finally, like anywhere else in the US, this state has numerous fast food outlets – anything from fish and chips to hamburgers and *tacos* – for quick and inexpensive options.

SHOPPING

Of course you can find anything and everything to buy in California, whether you choose to browse in major department stores, boutiques, shopping malls or main street shops in smaller towns.

The following are among the most not-to-be-missed (see also **What to See** sections):

Bazaar del Mundo is in the Old Town district of San Diego where boutiques and craft shops are now located. Note the strong Spanish/Mexican influences on goods in this 'birthplace of California'. While in San Diego, shop at Squiboh Square and on the outskirts of the quarter.

The Cannery is a multi-level shopping complex that covers half a block of San Francisco's waterfront. It was converted from a fruit and vegetable canning plant in the 1960s. Nowadays, chic boutiques and eating places surround a pleasant central courtyard.

Chinatown in San Francisco brims with things Oriental. Its main thoroughfare is Grant Avenue.

Embarcadero Center is the name given to the 8½ acres (3.5 hectares) of shopping malls between San Francisco's financial district and waterfront. Around noon you'll find many stalls selling leather items and jewellery.

El Paseo in Palm Desert, one of the satellite communities of Palm Springs, is known as the Rodeo Drive of the desert because of its high-priced boutiques. It is a beautiful 2-mile (3km)-long street lined with exclusive stores and art galleries. It is well worth looking at but shopping here will make a dent in the wallet.

Fisherman's Village at Marina del Rey, on the edge of Los Angeles, has been designed to simulate a New England fishing village. It is a good place to look for small gift items. Not far away, at the Venice edge of Marina del Rey, is Port of Craft, where a cluster of shops specialise in arts and crafts.

Ghirardelli Square, like The Cannery, is a converted San Francisco waterfront complex (it used to be a chocolate factory). The goods sold from its multi-levels come from all over the world. Also top-quality dining.

Lido Village at Newport Beach, south of Los Angeles, boasts rows of smart shops which open onto brick walkways or front onto the wharf. Also visit Cannery Village, which stretches for five blocks and includes artists' stalls.

Olvera Street, at the heart of downtown Los Angeles, is a pedestrianised Mexican market-place with shops, cafés and entertainment.

Pier 39, on the waterfront of San Francisco, is a bustling shopping complex, rebuilt with the wood from other demolished piers.

Ports O'Call Village, in San Pedro (LA), offers a combination of Mediterranean seaport atmosphere and colonial-style stores and taverns, plus harbour cruises.

Rodeo Drive, at the core of Beverly Hills, is patronised by the rich and famous. Its elegant shops sell prestigious labels at very high prices.

Shopping in America has always been an experience, either in covered multi-storey complexes which are filled with greenery and specially designed to be light and airy, or in clever conversions or 'themed' complexes, perhaps with a nautical or colonial emphasis. The latter are, of course, where you'll find unique boutiques and gift shops, art galleries and collectable items.
Something else the US has generally got right is its museum shops. Though some of the items may well be 'kitsch', you'll probably be surprised at some of the unusual pieces that are displayed, and, naturally, that goes for prints and posters as well. Theme parks, too, all sell gifts, some the fairground kind, but some, such as Disneyland's soft toys, are excellent buys as presents.
Large department stores also have their charm especially if you have time to sift through the array of goods. Frequent sales and discount offers can result in a bargain if you're careful and choosey. American-made clothing is generally available in a wide range of sizes (usually varying slightly from the equivalent British size) and colours, and American designer labels are obviously cheaper than when purchased in other parts of the world.
Also don't skip the sportswear shops at golf and tennis resorts.

ACCOMMODATION

The range of accommodation in California is as good as, if not better than, in any other state. There are many prestigious properties but there are just as many chain hotels/motels in the popular areas and along the highways. Names to look for offering good value for money include Quality Inn, Howard Johnson, Holiday Inn, Motel 6, TraveLodge and Vagabond. Visitors will find resort hotels with every facility on site in holiday areas like the Desert Communities close to Palm Springs. They will also find rustic lodge accommodation (as well as campsites) in parks such as Yosemite, and cosy small inns at destinations like Carmel and around the wine valleys of Napa and Sonoma. Holiday apartments are available for those interested in self-catering – the greatest choice is in the beach areas. And for those who enjoy the idea of bed and breakfast, there are plenty of delightful privately owned guest houses.

NIGHTLIFE

There is no lack of nightlife in the big cities, where anything goes from strip joints to symphony orchestras. The best way to find out what's currently on where is (a) to ask at your hotel, (b) to look at any visitor publications that might be in your hotel room or (c) to obtain details from the visitor information centres: San Francisco, the lower level of Hallidie Plaza, 900 Market St, tel: (415) 391 2000;

Los Angeles, 685 S Figueroa St,
tel: (213) 689 8822;
San Diego Horton Plaza, tel:
(619) 236 1212;
Palm Springs 2781 N, Palm
Canyon Drive, tel: (619) 778
8418.

WEATHER AND WHEN TO GO

California has its share of sun,
and usually accepts casual
dress everywhere, though top
hotels and restaurants may
require jackets and ties for
dining and may have rules
about no bare feet or
beachwear in their lobby. But
the state's climate is extremely
variable and how you dress
may well depend on your
destination. San Francisco, for
example, can be cool and rainy,
whilst Los Angeles and southern
California may be hot and sticky.
Desert areas can have summer
temperatures of well over 100
degrees F (40 degrees C);
mountain areas on the other
hand can get really chilly.

FESTIVALS AND EVENTS

January
Pasadena (LA) – Tournament of
Roses Parade and games

February
Los Angeles and San Francisco
– Chinese New Year
Monterey – Film Festival

March

Long Beach (LA) –
Congressional Cup Sailing Race
Monterey – wine festival
Santa Cruz – jazz festival

April

Long Beach (LA) – Grand Prix
Red Bluff – rodeo and parade
Santa Barbara – Arts Festival

May

Healdsburg – Russian River
Winefest; food and crafts
Sacramento – Dixieland Jazz
Jubilee
San Luis Obispo – La Fiesta;
food, music, entertainment

June

Mammoth Lakes – motocross at
its best
St Helena – Napa Valley wine
auction
Tuolumne (Yosemite) – Lumber
Jubilee with parade and games

July

San José – arts festival
Many areas celebrate 4 July in a
variety of ways

August

Sacramento – State Fair
Sonoma – county wine
showcase and auction

September

Sonoma – Vintage Festival with
tastings and re-enactment of
'Bear Flag Revolt'

October

San Francisco – Grand National
Livestock Exposition; rodeo and
horse show

November

Hollywood (LA) – Christmas
parade

CHILDREN

One thing is for sure,
youngsters will have plenty to
keep them amused in
California. If they are too young
to appreciate culture, they
won't be too young for the
plethora of waxwork museums,
laser shows, sea-aquariums
and theme parks.
San Diego's zoo is one of the
best in the country, but other
wildlife and safari parks are
dotted throughout the state.
American theme parks are,
without doubt, the best in the
world. Disneyland is tops, of
course, but there are others
like Six Flags Magic Mountain
and Knott's Berry Farm within
driving distance of Los
Angeles, plus Paramount's
Great America to the south of
San Francisco.
Few chain motels charge for
under 12's sharing a room;
coffee shops and fast food
outlets often list a children's
menu.

HOW TO BE A LOCAL

'Laid back' may sound like an
old fashioned cliché when used
in the 90s but it has remained
the key phrase for life – and
style – in California. If you can
relax, shrug your shoulders
and enjoy life, feel comfortable
wearing shorts and are
adaptable, you are well on your
way to feeling like a local.
Although the pace of life in Los
Angeles is frantic, on the whole
Californians are less rushed
than their East Coast
counterparts. Thanks to their
weather and their ocean
boundary, they are sun-loving,

fun-loving Americans whose weekends tend to be spent on the beach. While San Franciscans love their public transportation, the residents of Los Angeles would think you crazy if you told them you planned to see the city on foot. There's a star quality about the people who tend to feel if you've got it, flaunt it. Californians love freedom of action and thought, which is why they're first in line for anything that's novel and different. Perhaps it's a child-like quality that makes them pace setters for the frivolous fancies that turn up with each decade. They've always been keen on individual expression, which is why the first homosexual 'marriage' was allowed in this state, and why funeral services for pets first became big news here. Californians love the outdoors, they may have tamed it and created metropoli, but they'd never knock nature and have made sure their spiralling highways and skyscrapers are at least belted by greenery. Their attitude and their architecture has become a style of its own – California living. Not everyone lives in large haciendas, but the local homes tend to be sizeable and airy.

The best advice is to be as happy-go-lucky as you can, offer a smile, admire the wine and yes – be laid back.

TIGHT BUDGET

● Self-catering is one excellent way of keeping costs down,
especially for families – Californian supermarkets are large and well stocked.

● Motels often offer exceptional value, especially on the highways. Many allow up to four people to share the same room for one price – children's age-range varies from under 12 to under 18. The better ones have their own restaurants or coffee shop and sometimes a pool.

● California boasts many 'all-you-can-eat' restaurants. A great way for the hungry to enjoy all for a fixed price.

● Look out for 'Happy Hour' signs in any bar when two-for-the-price-of-one drinks are on offer, and complimentary canapés are usually provided.

● Help-yourself salad bars are a feature in many establishments – come back for more without paying extra.

● California's good kiddie country – numerous restaurants offer a children's menu of food they like, or small portions at half price.

● Don't bother with an organised tour of San Francisco – it's cheaper to get around by foot or cable car.

● Make the most of free entertainment either in the theme parks or on the streets.

● Check when museums and galleries offer free entrance – some waive charges one day a week or month. Local newspapers, tourist publications and information centres will tell you when.

● Pick vineyards that give free tours and tastings.

● Opt for a family ticket to a theme park if there is one.

DIRECTORY

Arriving

At the time of writing, international direct flights operate into Los Angeles – one of the world's busiest airports and major air terminal for southern California, and San Francisco – major air terminal for northern California. Fast-growing San Diego Airport is also an international one, but most incoming flights stop somewhere en route first. Major carriers with international routes to/from these airports currently include American Airlines, British Airways, Delta, Northwest, TWA and Virgin Atlantic. Many of them offer fly/drive programmes. Charter flights also use these airports. It is easy enough to fly between cities on shuttle or feeder service, but these short air hops can be expensive. Anyone planning short-leg flights, or adding California to another American destination, may be better off investing in an Air Pass (featured by most airlines) when purchasing their trans-Atlantic ticket, which allows several stop-offs and can be extremely cost-effective.

Travel Documents

Visas are required by all visitors to the US, except for Canadian citizens, or British or other European Union citizens visiting the US for business or tourist purposes, for a stay not exceeding 90 days, and provided a return ticket is being held. In these instances a passport only is required. However, rules at city gateways vary and visitors may not be able to enter the US from Canada without a visa unless entering by an airline participating in the 'no-visa' programme. It is best to double check the requirements for specific holiday plans before departure. The type and validity of US visas vary considerably and information should be sought from the nearest US Embassy or Consulate. The Americans are quite strict in these matters and passengers whose travel documents are not in order will not be accepted for travel in the US.

Camping

All the natural scenic areas boast well run camp sites which include good facilities. Especially recommended are those in the national parks such as Lassen Volcanic Park, Redwood, Sequoia and King's Canyon, Death Valley and Yosemite. Some parks impose camping limits of 7 to 15 days in summer (winter in desert areas). For some beach parks and parks near major urban areas reservations are required in summer and at weekends. Camping in undesignated areas is prohibited. Further information on state park campsites (including reservations up to eight weeks in advance) can be obtained by writing to: Reservations, California Department of Parks and Recreation, PO Box 942896, Sacramento, CA 94296.

Car Hire
(See **Domestic Travel, Driving**)

Chauffeur–Driven Cars
Easy to arrange, but expensive. Some hotels, especially the higher class ones, provide a complimentary limousine service to and from airports and some attractions. From the international airports there is a 'public' limousine service – these perform a shuttle service from airport to hotel at less than the cost of a taxi. These airport limousines are not to be confused with the luxurious private limousine. Bookings for chauffeur drive for US destinations may be made before you leave home through certain car rental companies.

Crime
California is certainly not crime free and drugs are a problem, but exercise due caution in the major cities and resorts, especially in the downtown areas, and you should be safe. In an emergency dial 911 and ask for police, fire or ambulance.

Customs Regulations
Non-US residents may bring in up to one litre of alcoholic beverages (if aged 21 or older), 200 cigarettes (or 100 cigars or 3lbs (1.4kg) of tobacco) plus up to $100 worth of gifts – duty free. There is no limit to the amount of currency (US or foreign) brought into America but arriving or departing passengers must report to US Customs all money in excess of $10,000 or its equivalent. Not allowed: drugs (other than prescribed), fresh meat, fruit, plants.

Cycling
With its 'near perfect' climate, California is a cyclist's paradise. In the city, and through the natural beauty of the state, cycle paths are in evidence, most of them well laid-out. Two popular routes are Sunset Bikeway on the outskirts of San Francisco, and the larger scale Pacific Coast Bikecentennial Route, covering the entire central coast area. It is easy to hire a bicycle, bicycle rental agencies abound (look in Yellow Pages), and most of the public transport systems allow bikes.

Domestic Travel
Driving
You need only a valid driving licence from your country to rent a car in California, though an International Drivers' Permit is sometimes required of visitors from certain countries. Most car rental companies require the driver to be at least 21, though some companies will rent to drivers of only 18. Touring California by car is certainly one of the best ways of seeing this varied state. Major roads are well-surfaced, wide and well signposted. Local roads are not so well surfaced and are often narrow. The American terminology is freeways, or interstate roads, for motorways, while other roads are collectively known as highways. In California they are free of charge (with the exception of toll bridges).

Petrol is about $1.50 per US gallon (0.83 UK gallon). The national speed limit is 55 miles (88km) per hour but is 65 miles (105km) per hour on some freeways in California. On city highways and in congested areas it is generally between 25-35 miles (40-56km) per hour. Road signs indicate specific limits which are strictly enforced – so are *minimum* speed limits on city freeways. And a word of warning about driving in Los Angeles – it has the world's most extensive road system, so plan your route AHEAD and avoid the rush hour.

If you are planning on renting a car, consider before you go the fly/drive programmes that many airlines offer. Sometimes a car is even included in the holiday package. Otherwise most of the major car rental companies have offices throughout the state – if a rental company has an office in your own country you can arrange to pick up a car from a US destination before you depart. Charges vary depending upon size of car, locale and time of year, and sometimes in pre-departure booking arrangements, but reckon on a price range of $30–50.

Bus

Greyhound Lines operates an inter-city service within California. Anyone considering using this mode of transport should think about purchasing an Ameripass (only available outside the US, passes are for 7 days, 15 days or 30 days – prices are in the local currency of the country in which the Ameripass is purchased). Unlimited daily extensions to these periods are available at the time of purchase. These passes enable visitors to travel anywhere over Greyhound's entire route system. Within the state, local communities and the major cities are served by local bus services. San Francisco in addition has cable cars operating across the downtown area (flat fare $2) and the modern BART train system covering the Bay area. San Diego has a trolley car service through the downtown area to the border with Mexico.

Taxi

Taxis may be hailed on the street but few cruise outside tourist areas in California, so if you are away from airports or major hotels it is best to phone for one (look under 'cabs' in Yellow Pages). Fares are likely to be from about $1.70 to $1.90 for the first mile, and $1.60 to $1.80 for each additional mile.

Rail

Inter-city rail service is provided by America's National Railroad Corporation – Amtrak. A special Far Western Region Rail Pass is available for purchase outside the US for 45 days of unlimited travel over the far Western states; children half price.

Electricity

The standard electricity supply in the US is 110 volts (60 cycles), in comparison with the more powerful 220 volts (50 cycles) of most of Europe, Africa and parts of the Far East. Electrical appliances from the latter area (or any using 220 volts) not fitted with dual-voltage capability will require a voltage transformer to render them safe for use. To avoid accidents these are best purchased before leaving home, though converter kits are available from electrical stores in the US. Also, electrical connections may be different from those you are used to at home. US sockets accept plugs with two flat pins in a parallel position, with in addition an upper, round, earth pin for earthed appliances such as an iron. Outside the US, Canada, South America, the Caribbean and Japan an electrical adaptor (different from a voltage transformer) will be required to run appliances brought from home (once it has been established they are safe for 110 volts power) – they too can be purchased before leaving home.

Health

It cannot be emphasised enough that arranging medical insurance before travelling is essential. Medical facilities are generally of an extremely high standard in California, as they are in the rest of the US, but costs are exorbitant. Insurance cover for an unlimited amount of medical costs is to be recommended. Service will be refused without evidence of some kind of insurance, or a deposit if no insurance. If you need a doctor during your stay, ask at your hotel or motel or look in the Yellow Pages under 'Physician' (see also **Pharmacist**, for less serious cases).

No inoculations are required for a visit to California.

Holidays

New Year's Day (1 Jan), Martin Luther King Jr's Birthday (third Mon in Jan), Lincoln's Birthday (12 Feb), Presidents's Day (third Mon in Feb), Memorial Day (last Mon in May), Independence Day (4 July), Labor Day (first Mon in Sep), Columbus Day (second Mon in Oct), Veterans' Day (11 Nov), Thanksgiving (4th Thurs in Nov), Christmas Day (25 Dec).

Money Matters

As a general rule, banks in California are open from 10.00 to 17.00hrs Monday to Thursday (until 17.30hrs on Fridays) and may open on Saturdays. They are closed on Sundays and public holidays although in some major towns and tourist areas hours may be longer. Currency may be changed at airports and some hotels, but it is best to go prepared with US dollar travellers' cheques (travellers' checks, in the US). The advantage of this is that US dollar travellers' cheques can be used very much like cash. Hotels, restaurants, petrol stations and shops in California will accept them as cash and give change where necessary (a useful way of topping up your cash supply). For this reason it is advisable to take out travellers' cheques in denominations of $10 or $20.

The American monetary unit is of course the dollar, which is divided into 100 cents. The usual coins are the 1 cent (or penny), the 5 cent (nickel), the 10 cent (dime) and the 25 cent (quarter). There are also half-dollar and one-dollar coins. Try and keep some small change ready at all times as some public transportation and telephones may require exact amounts. Dollar notes (bills) are issued in denominations of 1, 2, 5, 10, 20, 50 and 100. Be warned, though: all notes, whatever their value, are *exactly the same colour and size*. The easiest bills to work with are the $10 and $20 with a few singles for tipping. Remember that each American state levies a tax on most items so the price tag you see may not be the price you pay. Generally add on 7.25 per cent in California. Additionally, counties and cities may levy their own tax but this varies. You can of course use credit cards almost anywhere.
If you run out of money, look in the Yellow Pages for foreign exchange brokers or head for American Express. There is no limit to the amount of foreign currency you can bring in or take out of America (see **Customs**).

Motoring Organisation Benefits

The two motoring organisations covering California are the California State Automobile Association (CSAA) and the Automobile Club of Southern California (ACSC). They are both affiliated clubs of the American Automobile Association (AAA) which itself is a member of the International Touring Alliance (AIT). As such, the CSAA and ACSC make certain services available to member organisations from other countries. Check your eligibility to services while in the US with your own club. CSAA and ACSC offices are in most large towns, ports and airports and are able to offer travel related assistance upon production of a valid AIT-affiliated membership certificate.

Emergency Road Service

The AAA operates a nationwide emergency road service number. If you require assistance while travelling in the US, call 1-800-336-HELP. And if you are involved in a traffic accident where there are injuries it must be reported to the local police station.

Pharmacist

Quick remedy medicines such as aspirin are readily available at any pharmacy (drug store). Tablets containing acetaminophen correspond to tablets containing paracetamol in other countries.

Post Office

Some main post offices stay open 24 hours a day, but, as a rule, hours are 08.00 to 18.00hrs Monday to Friday and 08.00hrs to noon on Saturdays. Stamps for mail abroad are available from machines in drug stores – however, you will pay over the odds for these.

Sport and Recreation

Due to the equable climate, participating sports are more popular than spectator sports. Surfing, scuba and skindiving, sailing, horseback riding, fishing and in a few places, dune-buggy racing, can be enjoyed throughout the year along the southern coast. 'Fresh-water' recreation is also important. Commercial raft trips operate on some of the rivers.

Telephones

Telephones are located in hotel and motel lobbies, drug stores, restaurants, garages and in roadside kiosks. Exact change in 5, 10 and 25 cent pieces is required to place a call, except in the case of an emergency when you should just dial '0' for the operator or 911 for emergency services. For directory assistance dial 411. The first minute of domestic long distance calls, and first three minutes of international calls must be paid for before your call can be placed. California does have a direct dial system – dial 1 when the area code is different from the one on the phone you are using. To dial abroad, dial 011, followed by the country code, followed by the area code (minus the initial '0'), followed by the number.

Time

California is on Pacific Standard Time; in reverse of the time in Britain by 8 hours, Australia (Sydney) 18 hours, Japan 17 hours and Brazil (Rio de Janeiro) 5 hours.

Tipping

Service charges are not normally included in the bill – 15 to 20 per cent of the total bill is usually expected (more for dinner than lunch). Taxi drivers and hairdressers should be similarly tipped. Hotel porters expect 75 cents per bag.

Toilets

Public toilets, or 'Rest Rooms', are almost always of a high standard and are usually free.

Tourist Offices

Several offices will provide free information to visitors. The California Division of Tourism, 801 K Street, Suite 1600, Sacramento, CA 95814 (tel: (916) 322 2881) will help guide you to areas throughout the state. For information on northern California contact: Redwood Empire Association, The Cannery on Fisherman's Wharf, 2801 Leavenworth, 2nd Floor, San Francisco, CA 94133 (tel: (415) 543 8334). For more specific information, ask for the local chamber of commerce and information centres.

Whale Watching

From mid-December to mid-February the Californian grey whales swim southward along the northern and central Californian coasts. The return trip is made from March to mid-May. Cruises are undertaken by Marine Mammal Fund, San Francisco (tel: (415) 775 4636); Tides Wharf, Box 547, Bodega Bay (tel: (707) 875 3595); and King Salmon Charters, 3458 Utah Street, Eureka (tel: (707) 442 3474).

INDEX

INDEX

The Automobile Association would like to thank the following photographers and libraries for their assistance in the compilation of this book.

J ALLAN CASH PHOTOLIBRARY 5 Silicon Valley, 14/5 Street Car Museum, 20 Grace Cathedral door, 26 Street vendor, 37 Beverly Hills Hotel, 56 Universal Studios Hollywood, 58 Windsurfing race, 59 Balboa Park, 60/1 Sea World, 65 Hat Store, 69 Joshua Tree Nat Park, 88 Death Valley.

R HOLMES, Cover: Joshua Tree Nat Park

INTERNATIONAL PHOTOBANK 12 Tram car, 19 Golden Gate Bridge, 25 Sausalito Bay, 41 Hollywood.

MARRIOTT HOTELS 73 Desert Springs Spa.

MARY EVANS PICTURE LIBRARY 8/9 Washing for gold.

NATURE PHOTOGRAPHERS LTD 108 Long-billed curlew (D A Smith), 110 Mojave Desert, 114 White Mountains
(B Burbidge).

SPECTRUM COLOUR LIBRARY 13 Boat trip, 16 Chinatown, 22 Fairmont Hotel, 33 Balloons, 34 Pier 39, 35 LA skyline, 36 MacArthur Park, 50 The Westin Bonaventure, 57 San Diego skyline, 62 Spanish façade, 66 San Diego Zoo, 74/5 Napa Valley, 76/7 Vineyard, 79 Lake Sonoma, 80/1 Mission Sonoma, 86 Knott's Berry Farm, 97 Smith River, 105 Sequoia Nat. Park, 106 Yosemite Nat. Park.

ZEFA PICTURE LIBRARY UK LTD 4 Big Pine, 7 Mission San Diego, 10 Anza-Borrego State Park, 11 San Francisco at night, 17 City Hall, 27 Union Square, 31 Alamo Square, 39 Griffith Park, 44 Ahmanson Theater, 46 J Paul Getty Museum, 54/5 Fredericks, 67 Palm Springs, 83 Disneyland parade, 90 Lake Tahoe, 92 Mount Lassen, 94/5 Sacramento, 100/1 San Simeon, 102 Mission Santa Barbara, 113 Tufa towers.

Contributors
For this revision: Copy editor Colin Follett   Verfier Robert Holmes
Thanks also to the California Division of Tourism for their assistance